EUR⊙PE
ON A DIME

EUROPE

ON A DIME:

FIVE-STAR TRAVEL
ON A ONE-STAR
BUDGET

DRU PEARSON

Book layout and cover design by Kevin Boerup
Printed in the United States of America

Second Edition: January 2017

Cover: Ponte Vecchio in Florence courtesy of iStock photo

With gratitude to the three most important men in my life--

Joel, who always finds the way despite the odds;

Jackson, whose smile lights even the darkest way;

and David, who walks every step of the way with me.

To travel well you have to be well-informed,
not well-to-do.
--Eugene Fodor

Contents

Owner-Generated Sites Are Best
Sites to Consult in Order of Preference
Can You Believe the Reviews
Insurance
How to Find the Perfect Place
Ways to Pay the Deposit
Use PayPal

Before You Leave Home Checklist
When You Arrive Checklist
When You Leave Rental Checklist

Uber
Trains
When, How and Where to Buy Train Tickets
Train Travel Advantages
Train Tips
Carpooling

Advantages to Preparing Your Own Food
How to Do It
From the Grocery Store
From Local Bakeries and Delis
Assembling Not Cooking
Sample Menus

PART THREE

Is Travel Medical Insurance Necessary
How to Get Free Pet-Sitting
Resources - Gathering the Information You Need
How to get the trip information you need
Itinerary Planning
Never travel on a Sunday
Attention Anglophiles
Language Help
Packing Overview
Packing Tips
Essentials to Pack
Never Stand in Line
Free City Tours
Best European Car Rental Sites
Driving in Europe

PART ONE

To my mind, the greatest reward and luxury of travel is
to be able to experience everyday things as if for the first
time, to be in a position in which almost nothing is so
familiar it is taken for granted. - Bill Bryson

REASONS TO TRAVEL

I was born with more wanderlust than money. At the age of six I first saw a world globe and knew I wanted to explore every country on it. Unfortunately, most of my traveling for the next forty years was done vicariously through books and websites. Packing was a snap. But, oh, how my feet itched to get on a plane.

I craved the thrill of seeing places that had previously existed for me only in the pages of literature. I wanted to sit in one of those tiny cafes on Paris's Left Bank where intellectuals met and discussed The Meaning of Life. I wanted to see the crumbling old city walls, dotted with tufts of hardscrabble flowers that encircle European cities like a doting grandmother's embrace. Reading a novel about a chocolatier wasn't enough anymore. I needed to taste the chocolate.

If you feel this way, too, my book will help you realize your dreams and achieve the travel you've always wanted. When you begin to travel the Tightwad Way, I think you will find that travel will have the same effect on you as it does on me.

ALL SENSES ON HIGH ALERT

I find that being in a new place puts all my senses on high alert. In the early hours, when I meander down a street where the chevron pattern of black and white marble underfoot is almost as intriguing as the brightly colored shops on my left and right, I feel as though blinders have been removed from my eyes. Listening to church bells tolling a few blocks away, catching snippets of conversation in a different tongue, and sniffing a bakery's fresh-from-the-oven croissants is intoxicating. There's no need for caffeine on those mornings because everything I see and hear awakens every sense. It's so intoxicating, in fact, that just like a drug, I find myself wanting more and more.

Not only is Europe an opiate, it's also a living history book. Even walking down a street can open another chapter. Navigating the maze of narrow streets--some so narrow that outstretched arms can touch buildings on both sides of the road--I couldn't help but wonder why ancient engineers didn't take the easy way and build straight streets on a grid-like pattern. My Spanish friend explained that because city dwellers in medieval times had to be able to outrun their enemies, labyrinthine streets were planned with blind corners and corkscrew turns. The natives had no problem maneuvering the familiar streets, but their enemies were usually stymied. What looks like haphazard planning is actually careful engineering.

I had always assumed that the water fountains dotting Spain and Italy were attempts to ease the discomfort, at least visually, of living in an arid climate, but that isn't so. Because Spain was inhabited for 700 years by the Moors who needed to wash before they prayed five times a day, it was crucial that places to "clean up" be located everywhere. These fountains that today spritz the air with water droplets originally served a very practical purpose.

In the United States, we often do not sense the heritage of our forefathers. We are a relatively "new" country, and, as such, our roots in America are fairly shallow. But when I stood in the caves of Font de Gaume, in the Dordogne area of France, looking at paintings created by Neanderthals in 17000 BCE, paintings depicting animals that the hunters perhaps hoped to find, I felt a kinship with my ancient ancestors I've never felt before or since. To know that their hopes and dreams were depicted in the drawings on the cave as mine are on the pages of my journal was a connection that transcends space and time.

To travel is to discover that everyone is wrong about other countries.   - Aldous Huxley

DISPELS STEREOTYPES

Travel also dispels stereotypes. Before my first trip south of the border, I was warned about the lazy, untrustworthy Mexicans, but all I met were hard-working, honest people. The cashier at the little convenience store across from my hotel in bustling Guadalajara seemed to be at his post all the time -- whether it was 8:00 in the morning or 8:00 at night. I finally asked him if he ever went home. He answered, with a wave of his hand that encompassed the tiny store, that this was his business, he owned it, and so he didn't mind his twelve-hour work-days.

I caught the Guadalajara city bus one morning to reach Tlaquepaque, and was amazed when the bus driver gave me change from the open money box brimming with coins sitting on the dashboard. If Mexicans were as dishonest as I'd been warned, that change box would have been hidden.

I used to feel slightly sorry for anyone who wasn't born American for our country is the richest and most successful in the world, but my attitude has changed. I still love America, but I've realized that there are other ways to measure wealth and success.

In France, Italy, and Spain, the daily afternoon siesta allows the family to share a meal and an hour or two together before everyone returns to work or school. I'm sure business owners would make more money if they kept their stores open all day, but evidently they feel family is more important than chasing the euro. The government feels family time is so important that it requires all businesses to close on Sunday so families have one entire day every week to devote to one another. Europeans may not have bank accounts as large as Americans, but they may be slightly richer than we are in terms of time to spend with their families.

When I travel, some of my ethnocentrism disappears. I know America is a wonderful country, but I begin to realize that other countries have valuable ideas too. Europe's emphasis on recycling, with recycling stations dotting city landscapes like fire hydrants, shows how important they view the world's resources. Lights that automatically turn on when I enter a room and turn off when I leave remind me that conserving energy is important. When I see three-wheeled cars and trucks that get fifty miles to the gallon, I think about my gas-guzzler back home and feel a twinge of guilt. Stepping into a pharmacy in France with my usual walking-too-much complaint of a leg rash, and having the pharmacist spend twenty minutes consulting with a colleague and then instructing me on how to use the magical cream she sells me, shows me there are other ways to achieve good medical care. This is what happens each time I go to Europe; I realize all over again that there are many countries just as wonderful as ours.

While I am still delighted to call America home, I see it much more objectively now and know it doesn't have all the answers to society's ills. Europe may not have those answers either, but they have attempted solutions that I respect. Traveling has helped me realize that no country is perfect and all countries have ideas that might be worthy of implementation. I would never have known that if I hadn't finally packed that bag, bought a ticket, and climbed aboard the plane.

THIS BOOK IS FOR EVERYONE, BUT ESPECIALLY BOOMERS

The World is a book and those who do not travel read only one page. - St. Augustine

I regret never having had the opportunity to travel as a twenty-something. It would have been a treat to spend a year abroad, carrying a backpack, running all over Europe, and bedding down in hostels every night.

But my twenties are long gone, and once I was over fifty, I found that I needed a few comforts when I travel. And since even the lightest travel purse gets heavy after a few hours, I know backpacking is no longer for me.

BOOMERS DESERVE FIVE-STAR TRAVEL ON A ONE-STAR BUDGET

While this book is intended for all age groups because everyone, I hope, can learn some tips about traveling like a Tightwad, it is geared to the mature traveler. The one who uses a who-cares-what-the-original-purpose-was-bidet to soak travel-weary feet, but springs out of bed the next morning looking forward to hopping on the subway for another day's adventure. One who is content to pack every minute of the day with new sights and sounds, but leaves the late-night party-going to younger bar-hoppers in favor of a good night's sleep.

Perhaps even more importantly, this book is dedicated to the person of limited means who has never even seen a European bidet, much less put her feet in one. The would-be-adventurer who craves travel but is afraid a trip is beyond her budget. Someone who's looked at a tour brochure and concluded she cannot afford to go anywhere.

None of that is true. The purpose of this book is to show you exactly how to travel frugally in Europe. If you can afford to go to the beach for a couple weeks, you can afford to go to Europe!

This book is also intended for experienced travelers who want to travel more frugally and therefore more frequently. These are people who no longer measure success by the American Dream standards of a huge house, the newest model car, and a closet full of clothes--the folks who eschew material things because they'd rather be "rich" in experiences. When these travelers learn how to spend less money on each trip, travel dollars go further and that means more trips and more experiences. Rather than splurging on one trip every five years, one vacation, or even two or three, a year becomes possible. Why see only one country in Europe when it's possible to see all of them by traveling frugally?

As we discuss the ways both novice and experienced travelers can travel inexpensively I'll frequently use the word "cheap," but it will not have the usual connotation implying shoddy or inferior. On the contrary, I believe that traveling cheaply is the best way to see any country.

We have an odd notion in our country that "You get what you pay for," but that adage is not accurate. If you've ever read *Consumer Reports* magazine, the consumers' bible that accepts no advertising and conducts exhaustive tests to find the best quality merchandise regardless of price, you know that there is little correlation between price and quality. Often, the cheapest item tested is the very best.

So it is with travel. Some people think that an organized tour, run by such companies as Overseas Adventure Travel (OAT), Grand Circle, or Tauck costing $250-600 per day is a guarantee of quality, but I don't believe that is the best way to explore a country.

If you want to experience the culture of another country, it is far better to travel independently.

A true encounter with the culture means living as the natives do in the same neighborhood, frequenting the same grocery stores, and eating in the same restaurants. The fact that traveling independently is also the cheapest way to travel is an added bonus. I like to call this better way to travel close-to-the-bone traveling.

CLOSE-TO-THE-BONE TRAVELING

Travel is more than the seeing of sights; it is a change that goes on, deep and permanent, in the ideas of living.
- Miriam Beard

What does the Tightwad Way of travel mean? There are many benefits to this approach, but perhaps the most beneficial by-product of traveling frugally, is that it guarantees traveling close to the bone. Nothing gets between you and the place you came to experience.

Renting an apartment instead of a hotel room means you shop the grocery stores, dicker in the markets, practice your foreign language skills on the clerk who now welcomes you, after several visits, with a smile at the bakery around the corner, and use the subway system like a pro. The apartment, although cheaper, accomplishes what a more expensive hotel never can; it puts you in touch with the pulse of a neighborhood. At the end of a long day, as you arrange the flowers you picked up at the corner stand or have a glass of wine to toast a spectacular sunset, you feel as though you live here. Here in Paris or Rome or Madrid.

Feeling like a resident means you enjoy all the advantages of traveling like a non-tourist. Dallying is an advantage, not a liability. You savor every moment, sleep in late, run across the street to get fresh croissants for breakfast, take the leisurely route to today's museum, amble down the alley chock full of antique shops you stumble across on the way home, and get take-out for dinner. Living in the city, even if only for a few magical days, means feeling and tasting and smelling it. Slowly and completely. With all your senses.

When you "live" in a foreign city, you become intimately acquainted with its history. The first time I went to Paris, my inexpensive B&B was located in the sixth arrondissement, known as St. Germain des Prés, where writer/philosopher Jean-Paul Sartre and Simone de Beauvoir compared notes and wrote in the mid-1900s, and, later, the "Lost Generation" of writers and artists shared ideas after World War I. I was thrilled when I realized that the cafe, Les Deux Magots, was around the corner. Now I could go there and have a hot chocolate in the very place where Sartre and Beauvoir wrote, and where Hemingway and Fitzgerald bantered with Picasso and Gertrude Stein. This alone would nurture my soul and imagination for months.

After dreaming of seeing Paris for twenty years, the excitement of actually being in the city propelled me out of bed each morning before dawn, but I crept silently out of the house so as not to wake the other guests. My little room, a gold and turquoise Louis XIV gem that could only be reached by going through the dining room and across a terrace, was an extra that Madame rented only when the rest of her house was full.

The day I went to the Eiffel Tower, I used my guidebooks and city transit map to carefully plot my route the night before. Up at 5:30, I quickly showered, tiptoed out of the pension, stopped at my favorite patisserie to practice my college French and order a croissant, and make it to the Metro subway station before rush hour.

When I reached the correct stop, I climbed the steps to the street and looked around for the Tower. But it wasn't there. Only houses and apartments lined the neat streets. The Eiffel Tower was too big to hide, but I couldn't catch even a glimpse of its top. Evidently my carefully orchestrated route had a flaw or two.

A woman in a somber black raincoat with a de rigeuer scarf, the fashion accessory that only Frenchwomen seem able to drape so beautifully to frame their faces, stopped and smiled at my fractured French. She pointed to the right and suggested with a wave of her arm that my destination was several blocks away.

It had rained during the night and the freshly bathed streets glistened while steam rose from the sidewalks. Flowers decorated every porch or tiny garden while wooden shutters or little French balconies gave each apartment building a distinct personality. Every once in a while, the sweet scent of jasmine floated on the air. The only sound was the staccato-step of smartly dressed Parisians, surely the thinnest people in the world because they walk everywhere at marathon-speed, scurrying to work. This was a part of Paris I never would have seen had I not gotten lost.

Finally, across the street, I saw a tiny cafe with one

wrought iron table and two chairs set out front, an open door wreathed in ivy, and a chalkboard listing the morning specials. It looked so inviting I almost forgot for a second what I was looking for until, suddenly, there, just above the treetops, I thought I saw it. I quickened my pace and rounded a corner. Yes, that looks like metal filigree reaching into the sky. Could I be getting close? Ah, indeed, only a few more blocks and I would be there.

The line meant a forty-five-minute wait, but seeing the whole of Paris was worth waiting for. I lingered a long time, soaking in the view, and afterward sat on the grass to take in the scene, see the Tower from a different perspective, and write a few notes in my journal. The huge expanse of lawn, called the Champs de Mars, stretched for acres in all directions to create a fitting backdrop for the Tower. The greenery was as expansive as the Tower was tall.

My guidebook said the Eiffel Tower, originally intended to be a temporary structure for Paris's 1889 World's Fair, was criticized by the public who called it a "grimy factory chimney." Lying on the grass and looking up at the soaring structure, I tended to agree, though, with the Tower's creator who said, "The basic lines of a structure must correspond precisely to its specified use. To a certain extent the tower was formed by the wind itself." The Tower survived because Parisian critics eventually came to appreciate the landmark, not only for its practical role in telecommunications, but as one of Paris's most famous icons.

I was lost in thought when a car horn brought me out of my reverie. There in the parking lot was a huge tour bus disgorging passengers who walked a few feet to the Tower and quickly got in the elevator. As I sat there thinking over my morning and wondering whether to see the Musée de l'Orangerie or the Musée d'Orsay in the afternoon, I saw the same group returning, clambering back on the bus. Five minutes later they were gone.

I wondered what they would remember when they sat down to dinner that night. The members of the tour had probably paid a lot more than the cost of my Metro ticket to ride an air-conditioned bus from their hotel to the Eiffel Tower, but I thought my way of seeing Paris was more satisfying. At the end of the day, Paris would be under my fingernails, etched in every muscle of my aching body, and forever in my memory. Unlike the people who rode the bus and ticked off the stops on their itinerary, my Paris would stay with me always. It would prove to be that moveable feast Hemingway wrote about.

This is why I say frugal travel is close to the bone. By traveling cheaply, there's no insulation, no padding, no obstacles to get in the way. Nothing comes between you and the essence of the place you want to experience. The mundane, as well as the marvelous, is part of your day, every day. And that, I believe, is the way travel should be.

WAYS TO TRAVEL

While there are wide variations in each category, there are really only two ways to travel. Either you can plan your own trip--independent travel--or someone else can plan it for you--an organized tour.

There are pros and cons to both travel approaches,

and both approaches can vary wildly in price, but I believe there are far more advantages to traveling independently. And traveling independently the Tightwad Way is the least expensive and most comfortable way to go.

If you already know that independent travel is the best approach for you, please skip the next section and go on to Part Two. If you are still unsure, please read the following pages where we consider both types of travel.

ORGANIZED TOURS VERSUS INDEPENDENT TRAVEL

PLANNING

An organized tour means a company plans a trip for fifteen to forty people, invariably strangers who have never met before, who will be traveling together. The planners for the company decide what cities will be visited, what sites will be on the itinerary, which hotels will be reserved, what the duration of the trip will be, which meals will be included, and what price will be charged. In some cases, tours will also include air fare for an additional fee. If you want an organized tour, all you have to do is decide which tour to take and which date works best with your schedule.

This may sound ideal. You can simply pack your bags, grab your passport, and head for the airport. The problem, though, with having someone else do all the planning is that you do none of the work that helps you get to know a place. Without researching the area, you will not be able to choose the sites that would be most meaningful to you but will simply have to accept whatever the planners have decided you should see. Your days are scheduled according to what sites the planners believe are best for fifteen to forty people to visit easily. Of necessity, they must take into consideration bus parking, since this is the way the group is transported, and rest stop areas or restaurants that can accommodate a crowd. You may never see the slightly difficult to reach or somewhat isolated places that often reflect the soul of a country.

GETTING TO AND FROM THE AIRPORT

An organized tour will often include transport to and from the airport which is quite helpful when you arrive rather groggy after a long trans-Atlantic flight. To know someone will be there when you leave Customs, holding a sign with your name on it, ready to whisk you to your hotel is comforting. It is also reassuring to know that your guide will get you to the airport at the end of the tour for your flight home. Of course, even though the price may not be listed separately, the cost for this service is included in your tour price.

If being met at the airport is important to you, you can easily arrange the same service for yourself. Taxis abound at all international airports, and a simple search on the Internet can put you in touch with a reservation service. Or, if you're traveling the Tightwad Way, you can ask your vacation rental apartment landlord to recommend a car service. David and I did this for pick-up at the Rome Airport and were pleased when we saw Marcello standing outside customs with a placard. After almost 24 hours of traveling, we were delighted to know Marcello was taking over, putting our bags in the car, and driving us directly to the rental where we were met by our landlord. All this equaled no more than the price of a taxi we could have hailed at the curb.

There are usually much cheaper mass transit options available at international airports, too, such as the reasonable bus service from Marseille to the airport or the subway station located underneath Heathrow Airport on the outskirts of London that takes you to the city for about £1.90.

ACCOMMODATIONS

An organized tour usually arranges lodging that can accommodate a crowd. Instead of staying in centrally located accommodations that reflect the personality of the country, you will stay in large, fairly anonymous hotels. Again, the buses need a large parking lot and many guests must be accommodated. While tour accommodations are usually in three or four-star hotels, the rooms are comfortable yet sterile. They have conveniences like a concierge and room service, although you probably won't use either of these, but little personality. The ten-room 16th century mansion that's been transformed into a charming, if slightly quirky, B&B just steps away from the Duomo, the beautiful cathedral occupying an entire block in Florence, is out of the question for tour groups.

FOOD

An organized tour will almost always include daily breakfast and a few lunches and/or dinners in your total tour price. Breakfast is usually a fairly lavish buffet with lots of fruit, cereals, yogurt, breads, pastries, juice and coffee or tea. Occasionally, dinner is offered to tour participants at their hotels.

Unless it's a culinary tour where the cuisine is the focus of each day's activity, most food offered on sight-seeing tours is usually as bland as an airplane meal. Food rarely reflects the personality of the region but is created, instead, to cater to many diverse palates. For example, in Italy, you will probably be served Italian-American dishes, but not true Italian cuisine. The food is acceptable if not remarkable, and there's little room for exploration or experimentation as the choices are limited.

When you travel the Tightwad Way, you will sample all that a region has to offer. This is a topic that will be discussed at length a little later.

DAILY SCHEDULE

An organized tour keeps to a rigid schedule so that almost every minute of your time is occupied. While there is sometimes a "free" afternoon here or there, most days you are told what time to have breakfast so that everyone can get to the first site on time, how many hours have been allotted for each site, and the exact time you must return to the bus so you can reach your hotel that evening. The pace can be exhausting and frustrating.

You may want to spend an extra hour in Verona, Italy, to explore the streets where Romeo and Juliet once roamed, but you won't get the chance if the bus is scheduled to be in Pisa later that day. Your lack of interest in a tower built on an inadequate foundation doesn't matter to your guide. What's important is keeping to the itinerary so that all the previously arranged connections can be made. You will see what the planners decide you should see, not necessarily what you would choose to see.

When you travel independently, you decide the itinerary and the length of time for each site. If you become intrigued by the city's largest cathedral and decide to return later that evening for an evening concert, you can do so. Adding a museum that the tourist office recommends or removing a site that the man you got to know at the bread shop said wasn't worth your time is easy to do. Rather than rigidly adhering to a schedule that a tour leader has imposed, you are free to explore the city at your own pace and discover what is meaningful to you.

SIDE TRIPS

Every tour also includes visits to manufacturers. Tour leaders say that this is to give you an appreciation for products produced in the area, but I think the real reason is because guides try to bolster their salaries with kickbacks from the vendors. Whatever you buy results in a bonus for your guide. In France you may go to a perfumery or in Italy to a leather goods shop. If you'd rather spend more time touring Venice than visiting a Murano glass factory, you are out of luck.

Rick Steves, a travel guru extraordinaire whose travel philosophy is much like mine, does not think guides give you a chance to comparison shop; you never know if you're getting the best price. He says this about the visits to manufacturers in the "Plan Your Trip" section of his website: "...just keep in mind that the prices you see often include a 10-20 percent kickback [for your guide]. Tour guides are clever at dominating your time, making it difficult for shoppers to get out and discover the going rate for big purchases."

OPTIONAL EXCURSIONS

An organized tour will also offer optional excursions, usually at an inflated price. Some tour agencies tell you of the options in advance, but, just as frequently, the tantalizing options to see Rome at night or travel to one of the picturesque islands in Italy's Lake Maggiore are suggested to you at the first orientation meeting. This can be quite frustrating if you didn't include an extra $500 or so in your budget. The sales pressure can be intense because, as Rick Steves says in the "Plan Your Trip" section of his website, "Your guide promotes excursions because she profits from them." On the other hand, if you had planned the activities for your trip yourself, you would know exactly what "options" you'd like. Rather than spend the $80-100 surcharge with a tour, you could take the exact same side trip for a fraction of the tour cost.

NO WAITING IN LINE

An organized tour does, of course, hit most of the major highlights in every city and your guide will provide tickets so you can avoid the hours-long lines at the most popular museums and sites. For some reason I have yet to understand, tour groups are usually the first to arrive at a site; if you are not a morning person, you may resent having to get up so early every day (Getting up around 6:00 is the norm.) You may also be frustrated at finding yourself half asleep when you're seeing one of the wonders of the world.

What Tour Companies Don't Want Me to Tell

While tour guides will often imply that their expertise in snagging tickets resulted in your avoiding the long lines at the Sistine Chapel or the Louvre, the truth is that anyone can get these avoid-the-line tickets. The ticket or pass may need to be ordered ahead of time, but with a little advance planning, you, too, can sail past the waiting crowds and walk right through the door! And, perhaps even more importantly, you can make your appointment for a much more reasonable hour, say mid-morning or early afternoon, when the crowds of tour bus tourists have left. It's much more pleasant to visit museums when you don't have to push your way through throngs of other guests.

How Much Can We See

An organized tour covers a lot of ground in a short amount of time. Some tours require a change of hotels every night although longer tours try to arrange a two or three-night stay in at least one city during the course of the trip. While your luggage is carried to your room at night and loaded back on the bus in the morning, you still must do a lot of packing and unpacking.

Another disadvantage to this type of stop-and-go traveling is that it's difficult to know any area in depth. When you are rarely in a city for longer than one night, it is impossible to become familiar with the streets so you can explore a bit on your own. And it goes without saying that you and the bakery shop owner on the corner will never become friends because you'll never have a chance to meet him. Places that are of special interest to you may not have as much time allotted for visiting as you would like, while other places that you would rather skip might take all afternoon.

But perhaps the worst aspect of covering so much territory is that you spend a lot of time each day on a bus--sometimes as much as four to six hours. One of the ironies of a tour is that some days you're on the bus longer than you are at a site. This means you see a great deal of the countryside--but only through a bus window. I call this drive-by touring, and it's about as efficient at introducing you to a country as looking at photographs on-line.

When you travel the Tightwad Way, though, you are a traveler, not a tourist. By spending four days to a week or two in each location, you get to know the place in depth. Your pace is leisurely, not frantic.

MEETING THE LOCALS

An organized tour will often provide a "social" event so the group can meet informally with the people who live in the country. At least one prominent tour group catering to mature adults features a get-to-know-the-people-and-the-country activity where the tour group meets with schoolchildren, has dinner in someone's home, or visits a local market.

I can't help but wonder how isolated tour groups must be when a special activity is required to put them in touch with the people who live there!

I suppose groups are so isolated because they spend their days only with other Americans like themselves. They eat meals together, travel on the bus every day together, and tour sites as a group. Then, too, when almost every minute of their day is scheduled, they spend long hours on a bus, and they are so weary from having gotten up at the crack of dawn that they don't want to leave their hotel in the evening, I suppose such interventions are necessary. On a tour, there doesn't seem to be any other way to meet the natives except by an artificial "social" event.

When you travel independently, though, you are constantly interacting with everyone you meet: the landlord who rents you the apartment, the people you meet in the markets and grocery stores and shops, and fellow travelers on the subway or bus. Traveling independently means you become familiar with the country and its people on a day-to-day basis; no formal introductions are required.

GRATUITIES

An organized tour rather frequently requests tips. Not only are you required to tip (almost daily) the individual regional guides who have led you through a tour of the city or the Alhambra, but you are also expected to give a gratuity to the tour leader and the bus driver. A figure is always "suggested" and can amount to hundreds of dollars.

When you plan a trip for yourself and arrange for regional tour guides, no tip is expected or requested. There are few budget surprises when you travel the Tightwad Way.

DAILY COST

An organized tour costs anywhere from $200 to $800 per person per day (Not including the optional excursions or tips mentioned above. Tips and optional excursions could add anywhere from $150-$700 to the total.). A lower-cost tour uses mostly three-star hotels and does not include as many meals as the higher-cost tour where guests are housed in five-star hotels and all meals are included.

Assuming two Tightwad Travelers travel together, they will spend less than $98 a day per person in the more popular tourist cities, and less than $65 a day per person in less frequented parts of Europe. That's an enormous difference!

LENGTH OF TOUR DECEPTION

Some organized tour companies will bill tours as being a certain number of days long when, in fact, the full days you spend in the country itself will be two days less than the number listed in the tour catalog. The tour company counts the day you spend in the plane traveling to Europe and the day you are in a plane returning home as two days of the trip.

Here are two ways to check the actual length of a tour. If a company bills a tour as 21 days, note the itinerary details: Day One will say something like, "This is the day you fly overnight to London." Day Two through Day Twenty will list the hotels where you'll stay and the activities you will enjoy when you are actually in Europe. Day Twenty-One will say something like, "After breakfast, the shuttle will take you to the airport for the flight home." A 21-day trip then is, in fact, a 19-day trip unless you believe that spending two entire days on a plane constitute two days of touring!

Another method is to check the itinerary details. Look for days when you will have accommodations because that means you have spent a full 24 hours in that place. You will undoubtedly find that actual nights spent in hotels (meaning one full day in a country) will be two less than the number of days the tour advertises. A sixteen-day tour is actually fourteen days, for example, if you count only the hotel nights.

PRICE PER DAY DECEPTION

This exaggeration by the organizers of a tour--billing a tour as being 21 days long when it is actually 19--causes misunderstandings when considering price. A company will tout a 21-day tour for $6690 as costing $318 per day when, in fact, the real price for those days you are actually in the country, 19, not 21, is $352 per day.

When I calculate my trip costs, I consider only the days I am actually traveling in a foreign country. If I leave home and don't return from Europe until 35 days later, I calculate that my trip was 33 days long. The two days of flight time are necessary and must be scheduled, but they are days when I'm not paying for accommodations, food, transportation, or activities so they should not be included in my daily travel calculations.

Independent Travel Is Best

I suppose it's no secret by now that I think independent travel is the best way to travel. If you were going to a location such as Indochina or Asia where the language is problematic or you wanted to safari in Africa, then an organized tour might be the best approach. But traveling to Europe, which is familiar in culture, is easy once you know how, and there is no reason to spend exorbitant amounts of money to do so.

Although independent travel could be costly if you stay in five-star hotels and take taxis everywhere you go, the Tightwad Travel approach to independent travel guarantees you extremely comfortable accommodations, time to see every place on your list, efficient transportation, and delicious regional food for less than $98 a day per person (assuming two Tightwads are traveling together). That may seem unbelievable when you consider organized tours charge two to eight times that amount for the exact same trip, but I assure you it is true.

Fears Regarding Independent Travel

Sometimes I'll make a compelling argument to someone who has never traveled to Europe, and he will sound enthusiastic about traveling independently, be ready to find exactly the right apartment, search for a low-cost flight, and can hardly wait to get started. Then I see a look of fear come into his eyes because a "what if" has occurred to him. That "what if" is often the one stumbling block that holds people back, so, before we get to the Tightwad Travel approach, I'd like to deal with the most common ones in hopes of allaying a fear you might also share.

Do not worry about a language barrier. English is the international language used by air traffic controllers and pilots. All airport and train signage in Europe is in both English and the native language of the country you are visiting. Most Europeans begin studying English as a second language in first grade, so almost anyone you ask for directions will be able to assist. If you are unable to make yourself understood, you can always use an app like Google translate on your smart phone to ask a question for you. Guides you hire to tour a city or a museum will speak English. While it is true you will encounter a different language in Europe, it is in no way a barrier to travel.

Do not worry about public transportation. You will live like a native using the same transportation thousands of Europeans use on a daily basis. Getting around causes no problems for Europeans, and it won't for you either because, once again, all signage is in two languages--English and the native language. If you will spend an hour before you leave home using a website to acquaint yourself with the local metro or bus system, you will be able to zip around the city in no time.

Do not worry about waiting in long lines to get tickets for museums or attractions. As I mentioned before, it is easy to acquire the tickets you need before you ever leave home. These tickets allow you to "skip the line" legally, saving countless hours of your time. If you know how to use a computer, there is no need to spend a moment worrying about tickets.

Do not worry about ordering food or choosing restaurants. Because this subject entails a huge portion of your travel budget, we will deal with it at length a little later. Let me assure you now, though, that you will be able to enjoy the region's cuisine and never have to worry about ordering the wrong dish.

Part Two

How to Travel like a Tightwad

What I will present in the following pages is a step-by-step process for planning a trip that will guarantee you a reasonably priced flight, comfortable accommodations, delicious food, efficient transportation and all the sites you traveled so far to see. You may want to follow all the suggestions or only a few, the choice is certainly yours. I guarantee that you will save money by incorporating some of my advice, and, if you follow all of the steps I suggest, you will spend less than $98 per day per person. It will truly be five-star travel on a one-star budget. I promise!

What makes me so confident is that I have traveled independently or with David, my partner, on this kind of budget for the last twenty years. I know the steps work because I've implemented them again and again to plan trips for David and me that cost, in most cases, well under $98 a day.

Tightwad Travel is not a mystery; all it takes is a willingness to follow the steps that lead to a magnificent--and frugal--vacation.

Is the planning time-consuming? Absolutely. But

what you get in return for a few weeks' work is a personalized vacation that costs one-half to one-eighth the cost of an organized tour. You see only the places you are anxious to visit and none of the sites you would find boring. You travel at your own pace, sleep in when you need a bit of extra rest, and go non-stop on days you're full of energy. And, remember, close-to-the-bone traveling is not only the cheapest but also the best way to get to know a country.

Determine Your Destination

I have a list of must-see sites that I hope to visit over the next ten or fifteen years, but the order in which I'll tour these places is flexible. If the euro is currently at a record high, I may have to postpone next spring's visit to a particularly popular and expensive city in favor of a less-frequented and less expensive spot. If the pound is at an all-time low, I'll certainly make sure Britain is high on that year's list.

To plan your itinerary and get a feel for the costs in a particular city, consult the excellent priceoftravel.com website. On the homepage, you will see many price lists for places throughout the world. Use these comparisons to plan your next journey.

The article listing the total cost of a day's vacation in dozens of cities is particularly helpful. The day's expenses chart the costs for a 3-star hotel with mostly favorable reviews, two taxi rides, one cultural attraction such as a museum, three meals, and three beers or glasses of wine (Teetotalers can apply this allotment to another form of entertainment.) You can tell quite quickly which location offers the best bargains.

Of course, being a Tightwad Traveler, you will travel even more cheaply than the site suggests, but at least this will give you a general way to compare areas. You might have to postpone that trip to London, England, since a day there might cost $136.63, but plans for Sofia, Bulgaria, where a day is a bargain at $46.91, could be on this year's itinerary!

DON'T SEE EVERYTHING IN ONE TRIP

Don't be a drive-by-tourist. The point of renting an apartment and spending a week or so in each location is to experience each area in depth. You want an intense experience, not a scattershot approach, to the cultural wonders of the world, so don't try to see everything in one trip. And, remember, because you are traveling the Tightwad Way, you can afford to return to your favorite European cities again and again.

WHEN TO START PLANNING

It's wise to start your trip preparations as soon as possible. Anticipation is half the fun of any trip. Dream about walking in springtime down the Champs-Elysees or hopping in a vaporetto on Venice's Grand Canal; immerse yourself in books and movies set in the locale you plan to visit and brush up on the language you may not have used since high school. Share your excitement about the upcoming trip with your friends and relatives. Maybe someone will reveal a place off the beaten track that you would not want to miss or suggest a favorite pastry shop on a hidden side street.

There are also practical reasons for planning as early

as possible. You want to find the cheapest flight you can and that is accomplished by checking rates over a period of months. Trains in Europe offer cheaper rates if you reserve early, around nine to twelve weeks in advance, while the best apartment rentals are often unavailable if not booked months in advance. It is not too soon to begin planning a trip nine to twelve months in advance, and you should definitely begin planning at least five months in advance.

ARRANGING A FLIGHT

Remember the old days, before computers became commonplace, when a reservation meant a simple phone call to your favorite airline? Arrangements were a lot simpler then. Today you'll wait at least twenty minutes before you can even speak to a human being and then be charged an extra $25-50 if the agent makes the reservation for you. Luckily, making your own reservations online at the best possible price, while a little more complicated than twenty years ago, is not difficult to do.

As a Tightwad Traveler, you are planning ahead so you will have time to find the cheapest flight. It won't hurt to check the prices right now for your destination nine to twelve months from now, but do not panic if the rates seem too high. You'll still have plenty of time to wait for the best price to come along.

To gather information, use several sites. To get a general idea of prices for the major legacy airlines (American, United, and Delta), enter your search terms at Momondo, Mobissimo, Bing, or my favorite--ITA Software. ITA gives you more information about individual flights than you thought existed, but does not allow you to book tickets.

To find costs applicable at different times of the month or year, consider using Skyscanner.com. On the Flight Search page, enter your departure and arrival cities. In the date section, choose "whole month" to see the price projections for the coming months. Click on the date you prefer and a new box opens showing you the price.

Another price tracker is ITA Software.com. Click on Airfare Search. At the bottom of the Matrix Airfare search box, click Simple Search Options. Enter your departure and destination cities, the month for which you'd like fares, and the number of nights you want to stay. Click Search and a month of fares will be presented in another box.

If your preliminary search unearths a ticket that is budget-friendly, go ahead and book. While one of the third-party search sites may have helped you find the fare, it might be best to buy from the airline itself. Buying directly from the airline has advantages because it means you will receive credit for frequent flier miles and that's an advantage you won't want to pass up. Also, should a problem arise, airlines are more likely to help you if you bought directly from them.

Most of the time, though, you will not find a cheap ticket immediately, so you will have to set up a price alert notification; that will allow you to find the cheapest flight over the next several months. When you have an alert set up, you will be one of the first to know when there's an airline price war so you can nab the cheapest ticket!

There are a several sites that allow you to place an "alert" which means that you will be sent frequent email notifications about the price for your flight. If you choose to use Kayak, it is free to join as is the alert system. The alert you establish can cover a number of variables depending on the airport you'd like to use, the rigidity or flexibility of your travel dates, and whether you want to receive daily or weekly notifications.

In addition to establishing an alert for the major US airlines, it is also a good idea to sign up for the free newsletter of European airlines that serve the countries you'd like to visit. When these airlines have flash sales offering rock bottom prices--$599 round-trip flights to Europe from the US--you will be the first to know so you can quickly snag a deal.

Here's a list of the European Airlines which all make flights to Europe but often offer special deals for their "home" countries: use Aer Lingus for flights to Ireland and Britain; Air Berlin is a German airlines offering flights to Europe; Air France is a French airline; Alitalia serves Italy, British Airways is based in London; Iberia serves Spain along with Vueling, its low-cost alternative; KLM specializes in the Netherlands; Lufthansa is another German airline (one I particularly love!), Scandinavian Airlines (SAS) serves Scandinavia; Tap will take you to Portugal; Virgin Atlantic wants to take you to London; XL Airways is not well known but this company offers inexpensive flights to Paris (Today it's advertising a $565 round trip from New York to Paris.) from four gateways in the United States. Note that the only one of these airlines that does not offer a newsletter is XL, but it is worth checking its website if your destination is Paris.

After you've placed your alert and signed up for newsletters from various airlines, you can relax because all the work is being done for you. The websites will send you price notifications as frequently as you requested and the airline newsletters will tell you about flash sales. When you receive an email listing the right price, a week or several months from now, you can go ahead and make your reservation.

As I mentioned before, you may find it more advantageous to go directly to the airlines with which you have a frequent flier account rather than purchase from Kayak or any of the other consolidators. You will want frequent flier mile credit for your trip. Also, should anything go wrong at the airport, the airline may be more inclined to help you if you bought from them instead of from a third-party site.

There are only three rules to keep in mind when using airline reservation sites.

Please do your searching anonymously when you are finally ready to buy. Too many times you will find a good ticket price and will come back hours later ready to buy only to find the original price unavailable because the "cookies" remembered you and have raised the price on this flight you obviously want. However, if you search anonymously or use a different browser each time you search, you will find the cheapest price available each time. Two ways to privately search are to go to the menu in the right-hand corner of Mozilla Firefox and click "New Private Window" or use the browser DuckDuck-Go which does not track. You may also want to search your browser's Help section to determine if your favorite browser has a private search option.

Retired Baby Boomers have an advantage when it comes to buying because our schedules are usually more flexible. People who are still working traditional jobs often need to fly on weekends when their vacations begin, but retirees can fly mid-week when flights are usually cheapest. Be sure to check all the days of the week to see which is the best, but the cheapest day to fly will probably be mid-week on Tuesday or Wednesday.

Never forget to choose your seat carefully. Consult SeatExpert.com or SeatGuru.com. Running your cursor over their seating charts reveals the best and worst spots on a plane. On a trans-Atlantic flight, lasting six to eleven hours, it's a good idea to have a comfortable one. Also, do not hesitate to check your seat assignment frequently, right up to the day you fly, so you can change it should a choice seat--one with an empty space beside you--becomes available.

BID FOR LUXURY

As a frugal traveler, you will probably not opt to buy first or business class seats, but you may still be able to achieve space and comfort for just a bit more money by bidding for last-minute seats on two websites--Plusgrade. com and Optiontown.com.

Both sites work with airlines flying internationally to make last-minute luxury priced seats available. In a bidding system similar to PriceLine, a traveler enters his flight information and the price he is willing to pay for a seat class upgrade. Bid ranges are suggested on the site.

If a seat class upgrade is too expensive for you, you can alternatively bid to have the seat beside you remain empty on both of these sites. You will be notified within 72 hours of your flight if your bid was successful.

LOWEST PRICED FLIGHTS

Three airlines are giving the legacy airlines competition for inexpensive flights to Europe. If you are willing to fly without a few frills, you cannot beat the prices offered on Icelandair, Norwegian Air, and WOW Airlines.

Although these airlines fly from only a few cities in North America, the sales often include prices like $175 one way to Paris. Even if you must pay for a connecting flight to reach a low-cost airline hub, you may still find substantial savings. Go to each airline's website to sign up for their free newsletter that will notify you of sales.

While there may be an exception here or there, these three airlines will charge extra fees for luggage, special seat assignments, food, drinks, blankets, pillows, headphones, or entertainment. But, even adding $100 or so to the ticket price for extras, the total price would not begin to approach the cost of a legacy airline ticket.

To my mind, you are not sacrificing much for great financial reward. No one has ever written rave reviews about airline food, so why not pick up something wonderful before your flight and have a truly delicious treat on board. And, since my 5'10" frame is mostly legs, I actually like the chance to pay a little extra for a roomier seat. Water also should not be a problem for a Tightwad because it's always wise to carry an empty bottle that can be filled from a water fountain after clearing TSA screening. Want a cocktail to help you sleep better? Tuck one of those little mini bottles in your plastic 3-1-1 bag. Pack an inflatable pillow, carry a sweater or Pashmina scarf for a blanket, slip a book and headphones in your carry-on, and you'll have a comfortable trip at an unbeatable price.

To read the accounts of people who have flown these low-cost airlines, simply search for reviews at TripAdvisor.com or use Google's search engine.

FLY FOR FREE

I haven't paid for a flight in three years although I've visited Canada, Italy, and Mexico, as well as flown many times cross-country to visit family in North Carolina. My frequent flier miles have paid for all these trips.

I first wrote about the advantages of credit card sign-up bonuses on my blog back in January, 2011, but Travel Hacking, as it's now called, has become a way of life for many travelers. Dozens of websites and books are devoted to the subject.

Basically, travel hackers take advantage of bonuses offered as credit card enticements. Hackers earn the 25,000-100,000 frequent flier mile bonus by charging a specified amount--$1,000-5,000--on the credit card within a certain time period which is usually one to three months. After meeting the spending requirement and having the frequent flier miles credited to their accounts, they cancel the credit card before the annual fee, which was waived the first year, is due.

Since I use a credit card for all everyday purchases, from a pack of peanuts to a trip to Tahiti, I simply carry the card I'm currently using to meet the "spend" requirement, take it out of my wallet and put it aside when I've reached the quota, and then move on to the next card. I keep careful records so I know when to cancel. Within a period of a year, I had accumulated a quarter of a million points, but some hobbyists rack up millions of miles. I have read many articles by people who have flown around the world--sometimes twice--and never paid a dime for airfare.

There are some stringent caveats that apply to this hobby. It's important to use the card only for things you would normally buy, such as gasoline, medicine, and doctor visits, because buying expensive items only to meet the spend requirement defeats the purpose. While travel hacking is legal, only those people with excellent credit who can afford to pay off their credit cards in full each month should get involved. If you carry a balance each month and incur interest charges, you, once again, defeat the purpose of the hobby. But if you can meet those criteria, there's no easier way to earn free flights.

And if you are a newbie to this hobby, you are indeed fortunate because you can take advantage of many offers right now. A new rule, dubbed the 5/24 rule, that many banks are using states that credit card bonus offers are not available to anyone who has opened five or more cards within the past two years. If you are just getting started with this hobby, though, that rule will not apply to you and you can easily rack up thousands of points in short order. So, go ahead, and start accumulating frequent flier miles to get a free flight to Europe! There truly is no cheaper way to fly.

If you'd like information about the current credit card

offers and even more details about points, cards and travel hacking, thepointsguy.com and millionmilesecrets. com are excellent sources. Both sites have a "Beginner's Guide" section that you will find helpful.

Note that I do not include flights in my person/per day costs. While I can show anyone how to spend less than $98 a day in Europe for lodging, food, and entertainment costs, I cannot make flight costs a level playing field for everyone. Fortunately or unfortunately, where you live determines, in large part, the price you will pay. Location is destiny when it comes to flying. A flight to the same destination in Europe may cost $900 from New York City and $1250 from Portland, Oregon, and there's nothing anyone can do to change that. Still, I hope the information provided above will help you find the very cheapest flight from your hometown.

By the way, should you find an inexpensive flight, but worry the aircraft might be unsafe, be sure to check this website for a safety rating. Go to airlineratings.com and click on "ratings." You will find a rating from one to seven based on standard aeronautical safety standards and also a scale to rate the comfort level of the plane. Reviews from fliers are also included.

If you ever have difficulty with an airline and need to reach the powers that be, consult Christopher Elliott's excellent website section on company contacts. The link is elliott.org/class/airline/ Here you will find airlines' addresses--email and snail mail--customer care contact information and lots of other details you didn't even know existed. Should you be unable to achieve a resolution to your problem, Elliott will intercede on your behalf. Be-

coming a member of his site or signing up for his newsletter is free.

RENT AN APARTMENT

NINE GOOD REASONS TO RENT AN APARTMENT

Imagine waking up in your Parisian apartment in the
charming 10th arrondissement where the tree-lined streets
dapple the sidewalks with sunlight. You draw back the
floor to ceiling damask drapes and open the huge double
windows to reveal a tiny Juliet balcony where you drink
in the view before finally ambling down the short hall to
the kitchen.

Thoughts about the breakfast you're going to have
got you out of bed a bit earlier than your partner. While
he sleeps, you start the coffee for him and pour yourself
a glass of iced tea, congratulating yourself once again for
having packed a couple ice cube trays. As you squeeze in
a bit of lemon juice, you smile remembering the experience with the grocery store scale yesterday. Not realizing
the lemon had to be weighed and priced before checkout,
you had to ask one of the customers to walk you through
the process. You'd worried about seeming like a stupid
American, but your new French friend seemed to enjoy
helping you.

The fresh croissants from the bakery across the street
will go in the toaster oven while you scramble a few
eggs, adding fresh chives and a bit of diced ham that you
got at the market. While the omelet cooks, you quickly
set the table, putting out the freshly churned local butter
and the strawberry jam that's so good you could eat it by

the spoonful.

Breakfast aromas have roused your travel partner and he's now ready to join you for your first meal in Paris. Both of you sit, still in your pajamas, at the little table where the sunlight from the open window warms you, as you discuss what you'll see today in this beautiful city.

Doesn't this scenario sound better than the alternatives? If you were on an organized tour, you'd be rushing to get showered and dressed so you could eat breakfast before getting on the bus at 7:45. If you were traveling independently and staying in a small hotel, you'd have to shower and dress before going out to search for a restaurant that might or might not serve a delicious breakfast. Surely having breakfast in your pajamas is better than either one of those scenarios! But "pajama breakfasts" are just one of the many advantages to renting an apartment when you travel in Europe.

Be Part of a Neighborhood

When you rent an apartment, you will undoubtedly find yourself in a residential neighborhood. Unlike the streets around "hotel row," the shops, markets, grocery stores and restaurants that are all around your apartment cater to the people who live there, not tourists.

Assuming you travel to Europe to experience the culture and get to know the people, living where they do is the best way to accomplish true immersion. If there's a parade, a holiday procession, or a workers' strike, you will be in the thick of things, not isolated in a remote hotel. You can count on your entire experience being an authentic one!

MORE CHARACTER

Hotels are rather standardized; you know what to expect in the way of furniture and decor. The room will have the obligatory bed, nightstand, desk, bureau, and perhaps a table and chairs. There's not much individuality in a hotel, and the art is so standardized that most people don't even notice it.

An apartment, though, has more character than most hotels can hope for. Each is unique because it has been furnished for the owners who spend vacations there themselves. While you will clarify in advance that the bedding is sufficient and the rest of the furnishings and decor are pleasant, when you actually arrive at the apartment you may discover a surprise that will enchant you.

In Paris, David and I were delighted to find our apartment, in an historic building, had three floor-to-ceiling French doors leading to tiny balconies. This detail had not been mentioned in the description, but those windows added even more charm and light to an already wonderful apartment. We were also pleased when we found a scale tucked under the bathroom sink so we could track our daily croissant intake, and we appreciated the umbrellas in a stand by the front door on a day it rained.

The beautifully restored barn in Normandy boasted a kitchen that could have been featured in a House Beautiful magazine. We knew from the photos we studied before we made the reservation that the wooden farm table would be flanked by open shelves of colorful pottery and surrounded by windows with twelve-inch deep windowsills. But we didn't discover until we arrived that on each of those windowsills the owner had arranged a still life that reflected the French countryside--a nosegay of flow-ers, pieces of ripe fruit or a hand-made basket with a bit of gingham peeking out the side.

Our place in Fussen, Germany, with its glass dining conservatory and spacious living room furnished with antiques, also had stylized, etched walls that had been removed from a palace in France and relocated to this lovely apartment. The owner enjoyed telling us the story about acquiring the wall panels as much as we enjoyed hearing it!

I could go on and on, but I hope the point is clear. Renting an apartment gives you a truly unique temporary home that reflects the area you are visiting and may de-liver a pleasant surprise or two as soon as you unlock the front door!

Apartments Are Cheaper

One of the most important reasons Tightwad Trav-elers rent apartments is because they are cheaper than any other type of lodging. David and I have rented many apartments during our travels, and we have discovered over and over again that the cost, per person, for an apart-ment or house is half to a third the price of a hotel room. Even more amazingly, an apartment is usually cheaper than the price of a private room in what is considered, world-wide, the cheapest accommodation of all--a hos-tel!

I'll prove my point by telling you about the apart-ments we rented on a five-week trip to Italy and Spain, but I'll start by explaining what we discovered as we ex-plored accommodation options for Rome.

If David and I had planned to reserve a hotel room, we might have checked Expedia, Trip Advisor, Hotels. com and Booking.com. All of these sites listed the IQ Hotel among their top five. The IQ is evidently considered one of the best in Rome.

And it did sound lovely. The hotel, located close to Termini Train Station near central Rome, boasted a 15-meter double room with a king-size bed, Wi-Fi, satellite TV, a mini-fridge, desk, telephone and in-room safe. There was a large communal terrace available day or night where you could get a snack or simply relax with a drink from the self-service bar. Should it be too chilly to sit on the terrace, the bar in the lobby, which overlooks the square of the Opera House, is staffed at all times. If you had any energy left after a day of sightseeing, a gym and sauna were available free for your use. Sounds great, doesn't it? What more could you want?

What more could you want? You could want an apartment. We found a place five times the size of the hotel room for less than half the price!

Our accommodation in Rome was far more luxurious than the hotel touted by the travel sites, and it cost us only €700 instead of €1,595.93 for the week. Regardless of IQ, anyone can tell that's a bargain!

Our €700 penthouse apartment, with elevator, consisted of three huge bedrooms, two large bathrooms, a full kitchen, dining room, living room, a washing machine, satellite TV, and Wi-Fi. A balcony for romantic evening sunsets and a little studio with a desk for serious morning writing completed the layout. The location was not central Rome as we were in Monte Verde which is closer to trendy Trastevere, but the tram that whisked us downtown in minutes was literally right in front of the apartment doors.

In our little neighborhood, we enjoyed the open-air market next door where stalls overflowed with fresh vegetables, cheeses in all shapes and sizes, made-that-morning bread, fish fresh from the sea, marinated meats, and a hundred other items. The Frontoni Restaurant across the street had the best carry-out lasagna we'd ever tasted while Toni's Gelato shop was a mandatory stop on the way home after a day of sightseeing.

You might be wondering if the Rome apartment was a fluke, but I'm delighted to tell you that we found similar apartments to rent in every place we stayed on this particular five-week trip. In Florence, our home was a restored apartment in a 16th century building. Our one-bedroom apartment with full kitchen, Wi-Fi, washing machine, and windows overlooking a piazza, was in the middle of the city so we could walk to everything. It was €500 per week plus a €40 cleaning fee.

In the heart of Sorrento, Italy, we arranged for a luxurious two-bedroom apartment with complete kitchen, living room, TV, Wi-Fi, washing machine, and balconies overlooking the rooftops to the sea and the mountains for €100 a night.

Our least expensive apartment during this five-week trip was in Torremolinos, Spain, where it was off-season near the end of May. Our apartment there, a one-bedroom with two bathrooms, full kitchen, living room, washing machine, satellite TV with British stations, and a glass-window enclosed balcony located in the middle of this vibrant town was just €48.54 per night!

All of the apartments were just as they were described and we were somewhat disappointed with only one of them, not because of the apartment but because of the extremely steep stairs leading to the third floor (63 steps in all--Believe me, you would have counted them too.), and a very noisy piazza. We now have a rule that any apartment more than one flight up must have an elevator! Still, as is usually the case, we found that the apartments were even better than we'd hoped for.

These are the kinds of apartments you, too, can expect to find when you travel the Tightwad Way. Careful searching will always identify apartments or homes that are cheaper than private rooms in hostels. And with even a cursory apartment search, a couple will find that comfortable apartments cost far less than most hotels in the area while a large family or group will experience even greater savings with one place rather than several hotel rooms

Even when I travel by myself, I rent an apartment because it is so much cheaper than any other accommodation. I spent four weeks in Florence, Italy, studying Renaissance art at the British Institute of Florence and living in a delightful one-bedroom in a medieval building just minutes from the Pitti Palace, Elizabeth Barrett and Robert Browning's former home, the Ponte Vecchio, and my classroom for €500 a month. That figure included utilities and cleaning. None of the hotels, B&Bs, or hostels in Florence could compete with that price.

But you will also find many other advantages to apartment living besides price.

ROOM TO BREATHE

We are not small people. David is 6'5" and I'm 5'10" so we like to have enough space to spread out. If we rented a hotel room, we'd have to perch on a bed or sit in chairs, but an apartment gives us many more comfortable lounging options. We try to make sure that any accommodation rental we choose has at least two comfortable, overstuffed chairs--recliners are best of all--so that we both have a relaxing spot at the end of a long day.

Options are important during the day, too, of course. I always think the best thing to do after a long morning of sightseeing and a delicious lunch is to take a nap. David, on the other hand, believes the afternoon is prime time for studying maps and guidebooks to plan evening or next-day activities. The beauty of having an apartment is that we don't have to argue about who's right. I get my quiet napping spot while David can rattle all the papers he likes in the living room. Neither one of us infringes on the other's space, and, when you are traveling together for several weeks at a time, this bit of privacy and consideration becomes important.

And, since both of us are light sleepers, we appreciate the quiet found in an apartment. Unlike a hotel, rental accommodation bedrooms are usually located away from the street so we have no traffic or restaurant noise, and, of course, we hear no slammed hotel doors, elevator noises, ice machine racket, or voices in the hallway to disturb our nights.

GREAT FOR GROUPS

If you are traveling with children or if several couples are traveling together, it is far better and easier to rent one apartment or home than several hotel rooms. Each person or couple can have his own room and bath yet there is communal space, too, in the properties that cater to groups. It is difficult, if not impossible, to find that private communal space in a hotel.

You will also find that rentals are often better equipped than hotels for very young visitors. Since you are leasing a family's personal vacation home, the premises may be well-equipped for their own babies or young children. Cribs, playpens, and high chairs are often standard. We've even seen some vacation properties with elaborate playgrounds in the back garden!

APARTMENT AMENITIES

There is no maid or concierge service, of course, when renting an apartment but those are services you might not mind doing without. You might even appreciate not having a maid intrude on a morning when you want to sleep in. As for a concierge, I find that the owner of the apartment does an excellent job identifying the best stores and restaurants in the area, as well as supplying transportation routes, maps, and tourist tips by providing a notebook with his recommendations along with lots of brochures. You can count on a homeowner's objective opinion in a way you cannot depend on a concierge who may be getting a kickback from expensive tourist oriented restaurants. The homeowner truly knows the area and will direct you to the authentic cuisine that can be found in restaurants or carry-out cafes.

Your property owner will also likely be able to tell you about local transportation, the closest bus, tram or metro stops, and any other pertinent information because he likely uses public transport himself. If you will need a taxi to reach the airport when you leave, the owner will undoubtedly make arrangements for you.

While many hotels provide an Internet connection or a central computer that all guests are welcome to use, often for a fee, Wi-Fi is almost always provided at no extra cost in an apartment. These are usually secure connections, too, with the code provided when you check-in. Some landlords even supply a laptop for your use!

Perhaps the best amenity, though, is the one thing that can never, ever be found in a hotel room. The item that saves you money, time and aggravation is almost always included in your apartment rental.

What is this thing you will find indispensable? A washing machine.

A washer is a convenience for many reasons. Since airlines have such stringent weight limits and no one can take as many clothes as she'd like, doing laundry is a necessity. It's not a hardship to pack fewer clothes knowing you can easily wash them. There's no need to locate laundry services or make appointments; before you head out for a day of sightseeing; you can throw in a load of clothes that will be ready to hang on the lines when you return. Having once dragged my laundry down the cobblestone streets of Arles, France, where I spent an entire afternoon and paid roughly €22 in a self-service laundromat for two loads, I know you will agree that the apartment's washing machine is invaluable.

Don't worry about finding the soap you need. You will often find previous tenants have left a hefty supply of the local soap and fabric softener, or you can easily buy these products at the grocery store. Either use Google translate.com before you leave home to make note of the foreign words you'll need or rely on a phone app to communicate with a grocery clerk. You will probably want to buy fabric softener since most European rentals do not have dryers where you can use dryer sheets to take the scratch out of clothes. I also like to pack some extra clothespins and some sort of line I can rig up in the bathroom--just in case.

The washing machine itself will be different from the machine you are accustomed to in the United States. European machines are much smaller so they hold only half the clothes you might expect, and they have unfamiliar dials and words. You will be confounded by the choices you must make--water temperature, size of load, number of revolutions, length of wash and rinse cycles and so on. And there's no changing your mind if you enter the wrong information. Once that door is locked, the machine will single-mindedly do its job no matter how much you yell at it.

My first load of clothes in Paris took six hours and everything shrank because I inadvertently used the hottest water possible! I don't want that to happen to you, so as a precaution in case your European landlady does not supply instructions, I'm going to suggest you consult a website and make a few notes about how to use European washers before you leave home. It might also be helpful to print the diagrams. Here is a very helpful site for washing machines in Italy. slowtrav.com/italy/instructions/laundry_howto.htm

Here is a site that explains French machines. Adapting the Italian and French sets of instructions will probably help you use any European machine you encounter.

gherkinstomatoes.com/2011/10/11/the-perils-of-paris-or-how-i-washed-my-clothes-and-lived-to-tell-the-tale/

SAVING ON FOOD COSTS

This is such an important part of the independent travel philosophy that it will be discussed later in much greater detail. Suffice it to say here, though, that the second greatest expense after lodging is food. And what better way to save on food costs than by having a full kitchen where you can prepare your own meals? If you bring a few ice cube trays along, you can also cool your favorite drinks. Rather than spend $30-80 a day for food and drinks, you can spend $8-12 and eat very well indeed. I'll tell you exactly how to do this a little later.

WHAT IF THERE'S A PROBLEM

You will find most apartment owners are pleasant and cooperative. They will meet you at the apartment whenever you arrive (We've been met at 9:30 in the morning and 10:30 at night.), answer all your questions, and make sure you know how to operate all the appliances.

One of the qualities I particularly appreciate about rentals as opposed to hotels is that you can usually check in whenever you arrive rather than waiting for the afternoon. After being on the road for 24 hours and enduring an exhausting trans-Atlantic flight, the only thing I want to do when I arrive in Europe is take a nap. It may be 10:00 in the morning in London, but it's 3:00 in the morning for me--a nap is definitely in order!

If you must vacate the apartment a few hours before your flight back home, apartment owners will work with you to find a secure place to store your luggage. Remember, they are not dealing with the clientele of a huge hotel, so it's much easier for them to accommodate you.

Many people worry about what to do in case something goes wrong in the apartment. In a hotel, only a phone call to the front desk is necessary, but what happens with an apartment? Actually, we have had minor problems in the past and the solution is the same as it would be in a hotel--call the contact person. The owner has a vested interest in maintaining the apartment along with your goodwill (He assumes you will be posting reviews on the Internet.) if he hopes to earn a significant rental income. Because he knows it's in his best interest to deal with any problem, major or minor, in a timely fashion, you can depend on his cooperation.

CAN I RENT FOR THREE NIGHTS

Many people assume that unless they are staying in a city for at least a week they cannot rent an apartment. That may have been true in the past but no longer. More and more owners are renting for three or four-night periods, and I've seen many two-night minimums.

Of course, if you are staying for a chunk of time, you will often find small discounts for week-long stays and significant discounts for a month's rental.

WHERE TO LOOK FOR APARTMENTS

I won't kid you; this is the most time-consuming and frustrating part of your preparation. Finding the perfect place at the right price isn't easy. But if you are persistent and follow a couple tips, the hard work is worth it. It will lead you to the perfect vacation spot at a price that's cheaper than a private hostel room.

And once you realize how much cheaper and more comfortable apartments are as compared to a hotel, you won't begrudge the bit of extra time it takes to find the perfect rental. As Pauline Frommer, travel guru and daughter of acclaimed travel expert Arthur Frommer, said in her Complete Guide to Vacation Rentals, "Rent once and you'll never go back to a hotel vacation again."

COMMERCIAL SITES ARE NOT RECOMMENDED

I strongly suggest that you not bother with commercial sites. Yes, there are wonderful companies in every European city where the staff may personally inspect each rental, but, unlike a homeowner, the staff person has never slept in the apartment and may be unaware of certain features. When you rent from an owner, you are assured that you're dealing with someone who knows the property intimately.

One of the most significant drawbacks is that these companies charge more. Because they act as the liaison between the apartment owner and the renter, they must charge a middleman's commission. Someone has to pay the salaries of the employees, the fee for the Internet site, advertisements for their properties, and the office rent. That someone is you.

Still, there may be a time when you have to use a commercial site. If you must, here are some guidelines that will help you reliably choose an acceptable rental.

Do your homework. Trustworthy companies will be honest about the apartment's advantages and shortcomings. They will provide lots of photos and information about the size of the apartment, the furniture, amenities such as dishwasher and Wi-Fi, the location of the apartment, and the price.

Perhaps the most important aspect of a listing, though, is that reviews from previous renters should be available to you. A company with nothing to hide should be delighted to share its guest book with you. Read it and learn if what pleased or disappointed others will affect your vacation. If you cannot find this basic information on the site, or if a company does not promptly respond to your e-mails, move on to another.

There are many commercial companies vying for your rental dollar, so if you must use one, deal with someone who will give you all the information you need to make an informed choice. After all, your rental will be your temporary home in a foreign country, so your selection needs to be a good one.

OWNER-GENERATED SITES ARE BEST

As I said above, I think a commercial company should be a last resort, only to be used if you have no other option. I hope you will choose to use an owner-generated listing site rather than a commercial one. On these sites, owners pay a fee for website space, but they primarily take care of the rental arrangements themselves. The owner is the one you contact with your initial query, the one you pay when you arrive (Although you can often "pay" the company who will then forward the money to the homeowner.), and the person you deal with when you arrive to get the key. In some cases, though, the website company also makes guarantees for all the properties on its site so you can be assured of certain financial safeguards.

Most owner-generated sites operate this way but Airbnb does things a little differently. Airbnb requests your money in advance and then holds it until the company makes sure you are satisfied with the accommodation; only then will it release it to your host. Payment methods will be discussed in greater detail a bit later.

I believe owner-generated sites are better places for frugal travelers because of a few reasons. These apartments are invariably cheaper than those offered on commercial sites, because, as I mentioned before, there is no middleman to pay. Owners pass along those savings to you.

These rentals are not only cheaper, but on these sites you can rely on the accuracy of the information. The owner, who, of course, knows his property better than anyone else, lists his apartment, villa or house, plus a lot of supporting information. Here you will find a description of the property, a list of features/amenities, many photos, reviews from previous guests, a price list, and a calendar showing availability.

When you are ready to choose a rental, you won't have to deal with a company representative who may never have seen the place you've chosen or, at best, had a fifteen-minute tour. Instead, you will correspond directly with the owner who has chosen the kitchen appliances, hung the art on the walls, and selected the bed coverings. He will be able to answer any question you might have about the apartment, and, because he has used the public transportation himself, can tell you how to get around as well as find nearby grocery stores and markets.

SITES TO CONSULT IN ORDER OF PREFERENCE

There are several sites where owners list their rental properties, but my favorite is Home Away.com. With a million property listings in 190 countries, you are sure to find an apartment that's right for you. Also check VRBO. com (Vacation Rentals by Owner), a sister company of Home Away, because they list many European rentals even though they specialize in North American properties. Prices are listed in US dollars.

Listings on another major Home Away site are also appealing to Americans. Because the weather in the UK is so often dreary, the site advertising British-owned vacation rentals list thousands in desirable, sunnier-than-England countries! Since Brits and Americans often find the same features appealing in vacation apartments, this site is an excellent source of properties. And you'll often find that these apartments will come with satellite television broadcasting English stations. While the listing prices are in pounds, the individual page for each apartment also lists prices in American dollars. To find a British-owned rental at one of the sister sites of Home Away, consult HomeAway.co.uk.

Note that Home Away has sites all over the world: Home Away Italy, Home Away Netherlands, Home Away Norway, Home AwayFinland, Home Away Denmark, Home Away Sweden, Home Away Spain, Home Away Portugal, Abritel, Homelidays, Home Away FeWo-direkt, Alugue Tempoarada.

Airbnb is tied with Home Away for listings. This company, which has skyrocketed in popularity and is now a household name, is the only rental agency that is still an independent American company. Most others have been gobbled by Expedia (Home Away and fourteen other travel sites), Trip Advisor (twenty-four travel or rental sites) or Priceline (six travel or rental sites). Airbnb is the only one that remains independent.

If you're wondering how the site got its distinctive name, it all started in 2007 when Brian Chemsky and Joe Gibbia could not afford the rent on their apartment in San Francisco. In true entrepreneurial spirit, they threw three air mattresses on the floor of their loft (This is where the "air" comes from in Airbnb.) and designed a website advertising their $80 a night mattress with home-cooked breakfast.

People clamored for more rentals so Chemsky and Gibbia began the company that originally focused on shared accommodations--you rented a spare room in someone's house. Now, though, two-thirds of the rentals on the site enable travelers to rent an entire apartment or house.

Forget the air mattress (most rentals supply a regular bed) and breakfast (usually available only in shared accommodations for obvious reasons), but if you want a reasonable rental, definitely consider Airbnb.

And you cannot beat Airbnb when it comes to exotic accommodations. If you fancy a rental you can talk about for years to come, this site delivers. Everything from a castle to a yurt, and anything you can think of in between is available for a price. So, whether you crave a treehouse, train caboose, or teepee, consider Airbnb.

Airbnb has now gone one step further in an effort to become a full-service travel resource by launching Airbnb Trips.com in November, 2016. We'll discuss this in greater detail later when we talk about trip planning, but suffice it to say that Airbnb will not only help you find a place to stay, but also suggest spots to explore while you're there as well as provide opportunities for unique experiences to enhance your journey.

Since Home Away (along with its sister sites VRBO and homeaway.co.uk) and Airbnb have so many listings, you will most likely find an ideal place here. But don't despair, and certainly don't settle for anything less than the perfect place at the perfect price as there are many other sites to consult.

You may already look to Trip Advisor.com, an American company, for hotel ratings, but you may also want to try one of their vacation home rental sites. These sites have both North American and European listings: Flipkey.com, Vacationhomerentals.com, Housetrip.com and Holidaylettings.com.

Booking.com, owned by Priceline, has recently entered the apartment rental market. Now you can rent a hotel or an apartment on this site.

These independent companies originated in Asian or European countries, but do not discount them. The sites are in English, list thousands of properties, and often list more properties in particular countries than any other site on the market. Definitely consider Wimdu.com, 9flats. com, Roomorama.com, Only-apartments.com, Atraveo. com, and Casamundo.com

On all of these sites, you will find helpful features that will facilitate your finding the perfect place. There are filters allowing you to set your preferences for number of bedrooms, price, neighborhood and so on. Many photographs are supplied along with a list of amenities and a narrative describing the apartment and its furniture. There may be a diagram of the apartment layout and there will definitely be a map indicating in what area of the city the apartment is located. A calendar will tell you what dates are available along with the prices. Not only will contact information be supplied so you can e-mail or call the owner, but you may also be able to read a short autobiography that explains why the owner chose to buy this particular apartment.

The best item on the apartment site, though, is the review section. Here you can read what other travelers thought about the rental. While you will often find restaurant or transportation tips here, too, the opinion of other guests about the apartment itself and whether it lived up to its description is the most important advantage. These evaluations, written by people just like you and me, will tell you features the owner might have overlooked as well as drawbacks the owner would rather you didn't discover.

Never, ever skip this step of reading every single review for a place you are seriously considering. Use translate.google.com to easily translate reviews in a foreign language. It may not be until the thirtieth review that you discover the elevator is frequently out of service which means climbing five flights of stairs. You may also want to eliminate a rental if a noisy neighborhood means you will have to sleep with earplugs, if the water pressure in the shower is a trickle, or if the bed is as soft as custard. Reading those reviews is the best way to avoid disappointment and find a place that will truly meet your needs.

CAN YOU BELIEVE THE REVIEWS

All rental sites strongly encourage homeowners to seek reviews because the company knows how much travelers depend on them. All reviews are posted, both positive and negative; the owner has the opportunity on some sites to respond to any review rating the apartment inadequate, but the negative review will still be published.

Can you believe the reviews? There's been publicity for years about glowing reviews that have been submitted to rating sites by people who have never stayed at the hotels they write about. Indeed, there are evidently people who augment their salaries by writing fake hotel reviews for $5 a piece! In a New York Times article about these fake reviews dated 19 August 2011, David Streitfeld wrote, "As online retailers increasingly depend on reviews as a sales tool, an industry of fibbers and promoters has sprung up to buy and sell raves for a pittance."

There is no foolproof way to guarantee that every review you read about an apartment was actually written by someone who stayed there, but I believe most sites inherently have more credibility than hotel rating sites. Because only one renter at a time can occupy the premises, unlike a hotel that might have two hundred guests each night, apartment ratings don't lend themselves to deceit. The date the renter occupied the property and the date the review was submitted are both listed, so it would be suspicious if two or more reviews were submitted for the same dates. Also, reviews are published by the rental site itself, not the owner, so this is a safeguard against owners padding their sites with false reviews.

INSURANCE

The other reason I like these rental sites so much is because most of them provide insurance in one way or another. After you have read the next section in this book, "How to Find the Perfect Place," it is doubtful you will ever be duped by dishonest characters, but, if you still have any anxiety about renting, knowing that insurance is available may allay your fears.

How to Find the Perfect Place

Do a little preliminary research to find the most desirable part of the city for you. Remember that this will be your temporary home base for a while, so you want to make sure you look for apartments in areas where there are markets, grocery stores, and easy access to public transportation. Or, if you are driving a car, you will want to make sure you have free parking. Use guidebooks from the library or search online for these desirable areas.

You may decide to avoid areas that cater to tourists because the prices there are usually higher and you may meet far more Americans than you do natives. Don't be afraid to look on the outskirts of a city where prices are cheaper. The neighborhood on the outskirts will have its own distinctive personality and may be far quieter and less crowded than the historic center. If public transportation is readily available, you can be whisked into the city in minutes.

After you decide on a few areas in which to look, hunker down at your computer for a week or so. You may have to postpone appointments, and you may want to notify your friends that you are working on The Search. As I said before, this is the most tedious step in the process, but it is also the most crucial one. You'll want to make sure you get it right.

Filters

Start by setting the filters you will find on each site. You set the filters according to how many bedrooms you need, the price you're willing to pay, your location requirements (such as in the historic center, near the airport, by the ocean, etc.), whether you want Wi-Fi, cable TV, a washing machine and so on. Note, however, that the site may return some listings that meet most but not all of your requirements. Read the listing details to be sure.

Don't skip this step because having the correct filters saves you a great deal of time. There may be 1,852 rentals in a town but only 43 that meet your criteria. It is far easier to sort through 43 than 1,852!

Be sure to take advantage of the "favorites" icon if the site has this. After you have logged in, for free, you can note which of the listings are your favorites, and the site will save these for you so you can return to them later. When you are checking multiple sites over a period of days, it is much easier to look at your favorites, rather than wade once again through all the listings.

PHOTOS

The best apartments will have lots of photos--at least ten-- showing every room including the kitchen and bathroom. The apartments I like best have fifteen to twenty photos. If the owner has posted nine shots of the neighborhood but only one photo showing the apartment front door, pass it up. You won't want to stay there. That apartment must not be attractive or has something to hide. An owner who takes pride in his place wants to show it off and will post lots of pictures. Look for those listings that show you every room in the rental.

STUDY THE PHOTOS

The photos should tell you everything you need to know. Does the furniture look comfortable? Are there couches and armchairs where you can relax in the evening, or are the chairs spindly straight-back ones? Are there chairs and a table large enough to accommodate your laptop and serve as a place for meals? Is there a coffee table where you can spread out your maps, notes, and cell phones? Does the bathroom have a shower that requires you be a Houdini, or is there enough room to actually turn around in it? If the bathroom has a tub with a hand-held shower, will that be convenient for you? Will the kitchen meet your needs in terms of equipment and appliances? What about a sound system (radio, tape player, or stereo) and a television that receives English-language channels? Are there steps anywhere in the rental? Is the bathroom on the same level as the bedroom in case you need to use the facilities at night? Is the bathroom close to the bedroom or will there may a long hike in the middle of the night? Is sunshine flooding the rooms or does it look as though you'll need to use a flashlight during the day?

BED SIZE

One item that is particularly important is bed size. European bedrooms are usually much smaller than their American counterparts, and they have correspondingly smaller beds. Although the situation is improving, trying to determine the size of European beds is sometimes difficult because many owners aren't familiar with America's mattress terminology. If that's the case, you might ask the owner to measure the mattress. If the bed isn't close to what you are used to--152 x 203 cm (60 x 80 inches) for a queen or 193 x 203 cm (76 x 80 inches) for a king--you may want to consider looking for an apartment with twin beds.

Be careful, too, of the sites that are unintentionally misleading. An apartment advertising sleeping for four may be technically correct, but one couple may not want to sleep on a fold-out couch in the living room that is a few feet away from the apartment's only bathroom. You need to read the descriptions carefully. Remember, too, that bedding that might be suitable for children may not be suitable for adults. Bunk beds may be ideal for your grandchildren, but not for you!

Logistical questions will be answered in the narrative where the owner has described the apartment, its location, historical significance, if any, and other details that help this rental stand out from the crowd. This is where you should find the answers to most of your questions. Here are a few I always want to have answered: Is the apartment within walking distance of food shops and public transportation? Are there stairs or an elevator? Is there a patio or terrace? Is the apartment in a quiet area? Are a few kitchen basics like salt and pepper supplied?

Remember that the photographs (Again, ten is the minimum, and I love sites with fifteen to twenty) should document the promises made in the text. If you notice a discrepancy, ask a question. If the narrative promises two bedrooms, but the photographs show only one room with a bed and another with a couch, ask about that second bedroom. Or perhaps it looks as though that second bedroom can only be reached by going through the first bedroom; if that would cause a problem, ask the owner for information. Do not hesitate to clarify confusing wording because you want to make absolutely sure you find a place that will meet your needs perfectly.

The very best sites will also provide square footage and/or a diagram of the apartment's layout. If there's a diagram, notice where the bathroom is in relation to the bedroom, whether the kitchen is spacious enough for two to use at once, and, especially if there's no air conditioning, whether there are enough windows to supply cross ventilation.

STAIRS

If you have mobility issues or simply don't want to climb dozens of steps several times a day, make sure you clarify whether there are stairs leading to the apartment from the street and whether there are stairs inside the accommodation itself.

In Europe, the ground floor is what Americans call the first floor; the first floor is what we call the second floor and so on. If a listing is on the third floor that means you will climb three flights, not two, to reach the apartment.

And remember that the word "flight" is ambiguous as some "flights" of stairs in ancient buildings may consist of twenty instead of the fourteen or so steps we're accustomed to in the United States. Make sure you know exactly how many steps are involved and whether they are steep (I've been in some buildings where I felt as though I were climbing a mountain, not a flight of stairs.)

FEATURES

Next look at the list of features that are provided in chart form. Any question that wasn't answered by reading the narrative should be answered here. This is where you will learn about the items in the kitchen (microwave, freezer, oven, washing machine), bed sizes, number of rooms, what other items are provided such as toilet paper, travel books, and local activities and attractions.

PAYMENT

Look at the section about payment requirements. Sites vary, but you will either pay the listing company or the owner himself. Either a partial payment is due when the booking is made with the remainder due later, or the full amount may be requested as soon as the booking is decided. If the listing company is setting the rules, you will have no choice about how you pay the fee, but you may have more flexibility if you're paying the owner himself.

Some owners require a partial down payment while others insist on full payment in advance. If you prefer to postpone paying the full amount for the rental as long as possible, you may, if you've established a good relationship with the owner during your emailing, be able to negotiate this. While most of us prefer apartments that require only a small deposit as a guarantee, don't forget that it's better to pay the full amount if required rather than lose an ideal place.

When checking the section about payment requirements, also be sure to note whether a security deposit is required. If dealing with the owner himself on a Home Away.com site, your landlord may "hold" this sum in his PayPal account and, on your last day, he will cancel the transfer so the money is "returned" to you. Or, if you used a credit card to charge the security deposit, the owner will refund that amount to your account in a timely fashion.

If paying the security deposit to Home Away or Airbnb, the company itself will refund your deposit, assuming there is no damage, within a few days.

These are the ways payments are made on the two major rental sites, but all the sites use some variation of these approaches. The most important thing to remember is to pay with a credit card or echeck so you have additional protection from your bank. If you use PayPal, make sure the amount is charged to your credit card rather than deducted from your checking account to ensure that additional protection. More information about using PayPal is in the section titled "Ways to Pay the Deposit."

REVIEWS

After making sure that an apartment is exactly what you're looking for in terms of location, price, and furniture, read the reviews carefully. As I mentioned before, this is one of the most important steps in the entire process. Do not skip this step! Once you've narrowed your accommodation choices to a handful, read every single review, no matter how many there are. Don't skip the ones in a foreign language as they may have crucial information you need to make a decision. Don't forget to use translate.google.com to cut and paste reviews in a foreign language so you can read them in English.

The review section is where you will learn what it is

like to actually live in the apartment. This is where you will receive helpful hints (The washing machine works best with liquid soap. Avoid the expensive market next door in favor of the cheaper one down the street.), and candid evaluations about the comfort of the furniture and bed. Pay very close attention to any negative comments. Remember, these reviews are written by guests who have nothing to lose by being honest. You may think it would be wonderful to be in the heart of the city, but if a reviewer says you won't be able to sleep at night because of the noise, you may want to reconsider.

Look for places with the highest ratings, and trust the reviews rather than the photos. If a place looks beautiful in the photos but no one gave it a strong review, there is undoubtedly a reason and it's best to ignore a place like that.

I think it is preferable to rent apartments that have reviews because those unbiased evaluations can help you avoid mistakes, but there may be circumstances in which you have no choice but to rent a non-reviewed site. Don't be discouraged; maybe the property is new to the market or has had only a few guests who didn't bother filing a report. Whatever the reason, I would not necessarily rule out apartments without reviews, but I would ask the owner a few additional questions. Write the owner to ask if he has recently listed his place, or, if it's been on the market a while, ask him to supply references from past renters who might be willing to receive a phone call or email.

RED FLAGS

Avoid rentals with misspellings or grammatical errors in the listing. If an owner is that sloppy with his ad, he is most likely sloppy when it comes to maintaining his property.

Also avoid ads with flowery language that promise you the most wonderful place in the city. That person is probably giving you a hard sell for a reason.

Are details inconsistent? If the owner states his apartment is in the Marais district in Paris (Right Bank), but the map shows it is located on the Left Bank, be suspicious.

Are the photos cropped in a peculiar way? The owner may not want you to realize his apartment building is next door to a construction site.

If the calendar has not been updated or shows no bookings for the past six months, there is probably a reason the rental is being avoided.

If there is a negative review and the owner responded in a defensive, rude way, move on to another listing.

If you have narrowed your choices but cannot reach an owner at the number provided in the listing, scratch that one off your list.

Rent ought to be clearly defined. If the owner charges more for high season or "major" holidays, but does not specify when those occur, look elsewhere. Also make sure all fees including cleaning, security and taxes are clearly defined.

If the owner demands payment via wire transfer, knock her off your list.

SENDING A QUERY

Once you've decided on an accommodation, or three or four, it's time to write a query to make sure the apartment is still available. Although you've checked the calendar on the site, a recent reservation may not have been added yet, so you'll want to make sure the place can still be yours. This is also the time to ask clarifying questions about the beds, location, payment method, or anything else that you're concerned about.

Before you begin, however, please put yourself in the shoes of the owner. In order to be enthusiastic about renting you his apartment, he wants to know as much as possible about you. Are you honest, trustworthy, and considerate? He is hoping you will treat his apartment with respect and leave his furniture and art where you found it, and in the condition you found it. He's also hoping you are not an irresponsible college student who will invite fifty new friends to his apartment for a raucous party. He is hoping all these things, but he cannot come right out and ask you because it is against the law to discriminate.

That is why it is up to you to make a favorable impression and to let the owner know who you are without his having to wonder. Answer all the questions he would like to ask but cannot. Let him know immediately that you have integrity. Tell the owner indirectly that you are a mature, responsible person who will treat his property as your own. In other words, pleasantly answer the questions he cannot ask but wishes he could.

If you assure him immediately that you are honest and trustworthy, he will undoubtedly be delighted to rent you his lovely apartment and may work with you on negotiating the price. All of this can be done with your query letter.

I usually begin my queries with this line: "David and I are semi-retired professionals, in our 60s, who have fallen in love with your apartment." That lets the owner know David and I are mature, responsible people who appreciate his efforts in creating a pleasant apartment. I usually mention that I'm a retired English teacher turned writer while David is a retired ad salesman. That way he knows that we held responsible jobs and can undoubtedly be counted on to be responsible in regards to his property.

Most rental sites allow you to write one message that the computer "remembers" for all future queries. This is quite helpful because writing the same information and dates you hope to occupy the apartment can be tedious. At the same time, because you only have to compose one message, take some time to make sure your writing will convey your responsible attitude toward the owner's apartment. Double-check your spelling and grammar to ensure there are no errors.

You may end up with a query that reads something like this:

"David and I are semi-retired professionals, in our 60s, who have fallen in love with your apartment. I'm a retired English teacher turned writer while David is a retired ad salesman.

Can you tell us if your lovely rental is close to public transportation and grocery markets? Your rate mentions four people, so we wonder if there's a discount for only two people. Please let us know, and we'll be keeping our fingers crossed that it is still available for the third week of June."

This query lets the owner know we are mature professionals and therefore responsible and trustworthy. We are letting him know that only two people will occupy his premises, not several couples or a large family. Because we asked about markets and public transportation, it's clear we want to make sure we spend our money wisely, so perhaps the owner will consider a lower price which would be appealing to us, the ideal tenants!

Remember that there is a six to nine hour time difference between the United States and Europe, so it may take a while for the owner to respond. But within a day or two you should have a response to your query. If the owner has pleasantly answered your questions and you are confident this is the apartment you want, you can proceed by sending your deposit.

WAYS TO PAY THE DEPOSIT

If you can, use a credit card. It offers the most protection against fraud, limits your liability, and the transaction fee will be small. If you are booking through the rental site itself, this is what you will use.

USE PAYPAL

If you cannot use your credit card, and you will probably find that you often cannot since many owners are not big businesses that can afford the credit card fees, PayPal is the answer.

PayPal is an online agency that serves as a go-between for you and the landlord. Although the company was started as a way for small-time eBay buyers and sellers, who could not afford credit card fees, to handle their transactions, PayPal is an ideal way to send cash abroad.

PayPal is completely trustworthy, protected by Home Away's guarantee, and easy to use. David and I have used PayPal for hundreds of transactions (Most on eBay, but many international rental deposits, too.), never had a problem, and find it quite convenient to use. PayPal does not divulge your personal information and shields you against identity theft. If you do have difficulty, accounts and account owners can be traced; also, PayPal will investigate and retrieve your money if a dispute with them is filed within 45 days. Best of all, setting up an account is free.

One of the most advantageous aspects about using PayPal to pay your apartment deposit is that you can have PayPal use your credit card for the transaction (Be sure to uncheck the default bank checking account.). This gives you even more security. In the rare event of misuse, you would have the full weight of your credit card company's fraud department on your side as well as PayPal's.

So, all of this information should give you reassurance in using PayPal. With not only your credit card company, but also PayPal's considerable resources, working to resolve any problems or retrieve your money in the unlikely case of fraud, you should feel quite confident in performing transactions with them.

HOW TO USE PAYPAL

After you have enrolled for a free account--and note that it can take a week for all the steps in this process--send your deposit to your landlord's e-mail address or mobile phone number.

Here are the steps you should follow. Log in and click "Pay or Send Money" on the next screen. On the next page, click "Pay for Goods or Services." Enter the email, address or phone number and proceed by following the prompts. It's a very simple process. You will not pay an extra fee for this transaction, although your landlord will be billed a small amount. Your landlord may ask you to reimburse him for this nominal charge when you arrive, but the owner usually absorbs the fee.

Make sure the money is being deducted from your credit card. Often, PayPal's default setting is your checking account, so you will want to double-check that the money is being transferred from the correct place.

In the message section, type the details of the transaction. It might read something like this, "This €200 is the partial payment that also acts as a deposit for the Ancarana Apartment owned by Toni Ancarana, in Rome, Italy, for the week's rental May 1-8. The remainder of the €600 will be paid upon arrival on 1 May." This message serves to clarify for you and your landlord the exact terms of your agreement. If you're renting several places, these notes will also help you remember what's already been paid and what is owed to each owner.

Next, a receipt will be sent to your e-mail account. On this receipt will be all your information as well as your landlord's, your message explaining the deposit, and a transaction ID number. It's probably wise to make a copy of this information to add to your travel documents, and it's smart to save the message in an on-line file so you can access it from in Europe if necessary.

One of the best advantages of using PayPal is that your transaction is covered under PayPal's Purchase Protection Plan. That guarantee plus the insurance provided by your credit card's bank gives you more assurance than you get with most other transactions in life!

And that's all there is to it. It may sound complicated because I've spelled out all the steps in great detail, but it truly takes only moments to send cash overseas.

OTHER PAYMENT METHODS

I have never used it, but Moneybookers.com is another reliable online money transfer service.

If you feel you've established a particularly strong rapport with the landlord who is from your hometown or whose sister was in your college sorority, you might feel confident about depositing the security amount in the landlord's US bank. When I have done that, I've asked the teller to initial a note stating that the amount serves as a rental deposit. Then I make sure the landlord sends me a receipt that details the terms of our agreement.

PAYMENT METHODS TO AVOID

All the payment methods listed above are recommended by rental companies.

Rental companies and travel sites do not recommend wiring money via Western Union or MoneyGram, and neither approach is covered under any rental agency's guarantee. If a landlord suggests you use either one, do not have anything further to do with him.

CHECKLISTS

BEFORE YOU LEAVE HOME CHECKLIST

If using Uber or a taxi to reach the apartment from the airport, have your destination printed on a card so you can easily communicate with the driver.

Use Google maps or another Internet map service to locate the rental. Print this map and take it with you.

Make sure you have clear arrangements to meet your host. Know her phone number in case your flight is delayed. Have a backup plan in case she is unavoidably delayed. Is there a cafe near the rental, preferably one with free Wi-Fi so she can call your cell phone, where you could wait for her in case of rain or a delay?

WHEN YOU ARRIVE CHECKLIST

While it certainly isn't mandatory, it's a nice gesture to take a small gift to your host. This can be something that represents your hometown--I like to take a tiny jar of Arizona cactus jelly--or something you think the host would find useful. If you can't possibly pack another thing in your suitcase or if your town doesn't have any interesting gift souvenirs, consider buying a small present there. I once bought macaroon cookies for a host in Brittany, France, and was rewarded with a kiss on the cheek and two water color drawings!

Make sure you know how to operate all the appliances. Have the owner show you, not simply tell you.

If there is a TV, make sure it is "tuned" to the English language stations, if any.

Ask for the booklet/guide/or whatever she calls the information packet she composed that contains information about the apartment, appliances, public transportation, restaurants, stores, and markets.

Use the key to make sure you can deal with a front door lock that may be temperamental.

If there is Wi-Fi, make sure you have the code and password. If time permits, turn on your laptop to make sure you can connect easily.

Don't forget to clarify when and what time you will check out, whether you need a taxi on that day, and where to leave the key if the host cannot meet you. Remember, if you use Uber you will be able to arrange your own transportation. If you made a deposit, be sure to find out how it will be returned to you.

WHEN YOU LEAVE RENTAL CHECKLIST

If the host has a guestbook, do try to write a message. I also like to leave a postcard picturing my hometown with a message that thanks my host for making me feel at home in a foreign land.

After you return home, please remember to write a review. The host needs your feedback and future renters depend on your honest evaluation. Just as you found the reviews essential in choosing your apartment, so future renters will be grateful for your honest assessment.

LOCAL & INTERNATIONAL TRANSPORTATION

You're living in an apartment and shopping the food markets like a local in Paris or Rome or Madrid, so why not use local transportation? It's not only cheaper than taking taxis and easier on your feet than walking everywhere (Although I always lose eight to twelve pounds on every trip because of the extra walking.), but you'll also enjoy interacting with the local people.

Type these words in a Google search engine: "guide to (whatever city you're visiting--bus or metro) system" and you will get several results. You can also find information on blogs and in guidebooks. If you don't print the information before you leave, stop at a tourist bureau when you arrive in the city and get a map of the bus and metro systems.

If using public transportation still does not appeal to you after your initial research, you might consider using a ride-sharing service like Uber. Uber is remarkably easy, efficient, and inexpensive. Though more costly than public transportation, it is cheaper than using local taxis.

UBER

Here's how to use Uber. Sign up on the smartphone app, uber.com, before leaving home. You will register all the pertinent information and securely register a credit card number. It is best to use a credit card that does not charge foreign transaction fees. Then, when you are in Europe, using the Wi-Fi in your apartment or the free Wi-Fi at any cafe so you avoid roaming charges, input the information into the Uber app. The app will quickly tell you how much the ride will cost, and, if you decide the price is appropriate, it will show you a photo of your driver and the car that will pick you up as well as tell you how long it will take for the driver to reach you.

A car will soon arrive to whisk you to your destination. You do not tip the driver, but, instead, later assign him a rank of one to five stars depending on how pleasant you found his service. Uber will send you an email asking you to perform this rating. The driver will also give you a one to five star rating depending on your pleasantness as a rider. Since this service relies on ratings, not tips, you are better assured of having an inexpensive, pleasant ride than you might experience in a taxi.

Two advantages to using Uber in Europe are that you can enter your destination using your phone's app rather than have to communicate with your driver in a foreign language, and you do not have to worry about being short-changed by the driver because of fumbling with a foreign currency. Your credit card will be billed the appropriate amount you agreed to when you ordered the ride.

If you're still leery about trying Uber in Europe, Google "using Uber in Europe" to read about other people's experiences. I think you'll find the personal anecdotes reassuring.

When you do decide to walk, there are excellent apps for your smart phone that will help you navigate a city even without being connected to Wi-Fi. Try Mapsme for intricately detailed walking maps or Triposo if you want more site commentary. It is also possible to us Google maps if you will punch the "Save a new offline map" feature after you've found the place you want to explore.

TRANSPORTATION TO ANOTHER EUROPEAN CITY OR COUNTRY

Some people like to take advantage of one of the low-cost European airlines such as EasyJet or Ryanair, but there are inherent problems in using these airlines. The companies cut costs by using smaller, out-of-the-way airports, by limiting the luggage amounts, and by cramming seats so tightly together that a tall person has his knees tucked under his chin. By the time you add transportation costs to the remote airport, luggage fees, misery factor, and the time you waste getting to the remote airport an hour ahead of departure, you would have been far better off taking the train.

TRAINS

Unless you live in the Eastern United States, you probably don't use trains very often. Most Americans rely on cars to get them where they're going, and if they can't drive, they'll take a plane. Passenger train routes don't reach every town in America and, even if they did, trips across this vast country would be tedious and long.

This is not the case in Europe where it takes only a couple hours of train travel before you have to switch to another language. Taking a train is second nature to Europeans because it is usually the easiest and cheapest way to travel within a country or to neighboring countries. Unlike the United States, all of Europe is connected by rail. You will find bustling terminals located in the heart of the city with all the amenities of an airport or lovely rural stations in the midst of tiny towns. The trains themselves are extraordinarily comfortable with generous seating--even in second class--plenty of space for all your luggage, dining cars, and toilet facilities.

When, How and Where to Buy Train Tickets

As a general rule, if you are traveling to a nearby town less than an hour or so away, plan to buy your train ticket when you arrive. Go to the train station and either use the automated ticket machines which you can set for English language instructions, or wait in line at the counter to speak to an agent.

Most agents speak some English and it is fairly simple to make your request. If you want extra assurance that you've been clear about your needs, simply write your destination city on a piece of paper, the date (Make sure you put the number before the month because this is the way it's done in Europe. May 23 is written 23 May.) and indicate 1st or 2nd class. The train employees will be quite helpful, and you'll soon have tickets in hand.

In some towns, a travel office will be happy to make these reservations for you at no charge.

If you are traveling to a distant city, however, or to another country, you would be wise to buy tickets in advance because that is how you get discounted fares. These discounted fares are significant as you will frequently save 50%! The only way to get them, though, is by buying in advance.

Tickets for most high-speed, long-distance trains are sold 60-90 days in advance. It is pointless to try to buy tickets earlier as the routes and fees will not be posted. The exception to this is the Eurostar which offers discounted rates as early as 120 days in advance.

Remember, early reservations get the cheapest tickets. There are no "sales" as there are with airlines; a discounted train ticket can only be gotten by buying early.

There is so much information about buying train tickets that a separate book would be needed to cover all the details, but all you really need to know is covered in the next few pages. I'll mention only a few general guidelines and then point you to websites which will allow you to purchase tickets for every country you dream of seeing.

TRAIN TRAVEL ADVANTAGES

But first you may want to know why train travel is so wonderful in Europe. Here are the reasons I think you'll love it.

A train can take you across a country for less than a taxi costs from the airport to the city center! David and I paid €50 to the driver to reach Rome from the international airport; a train ticket on a high speed train from Florence to Naples, ordered three months in advance, costs only €30 at this writing.

You can take as much luggage as you like. Instead of being limited to one bag or being charged extra for additional bags as you are on a plane, the only restriction on a train is that you have to be able to hoist the bags into the train car yourself. Take one or four --the decision is yours.

You can keep an eye on your bags, too, as they can be stored in the luggage area at the end of each car, between the seats in first-class cars (But only if you have a first-class ticket.), or in overhead seat racks. You are the only one touching your bag, so you need not fear theft or mishandling as you do with airlines. At the end of the journey, there's no waiting for the airline to deliver your bag to the carousel. You just grab your bag and hop off the train.

Airports are usually situated far from the city center so reaching them can be problematic and expensive, but train stations are almost always located in the center of town. If you are renting a car, the rental offices are conveniently located at the train station, or public transit can cheaply transport you to and from your apartment rental.

You must arrive at least an hour early for a flight. Once you factor in the time it takes to get to an outlying airport, often 45 minutes to an hour, you might spend an entire morning or afternoon simply preparing to leave before you even board the plane. With a train, on the other hand, there's little point in arriving at the station more than twenty minutes ahead of time since the train platform (In a large station there are often thirty or so tracks.) won't even be listed until fifteen minutes before departure. This gives you extra time to linger over a last meal in the city, see one more historic site, or go for a leisurely walk before you travel to the next place on your itinerary. NOTE that the one exception to this rule is the Eurostar. The Eurostar requires a thirty-minute advance check-in, and there is a mandatory security screening similar to what one experiences at airports.

As I've mentioned before, David and I are tall people, so sitting in some economy airline seats can leave us feeling like pretzels for days after the flight. Trains, however, are comfortable. The seating area is spacious with footrests, pouches for magazines or water bottle storage, and enough leg room to satisfy 6'5" David. Unlike airlines where standing is not appreciated, no one seems to mind if you walk around or go to the dining car or bathroom.

Perhaps the best aspect of train travel, though, is that you can truly see the countryside as you travel. Even though you're speeding by at 200 miles per hour, these views are vastly preferable to the gray clouds you usually see out of airplane windows. David and I like to pack a lunch and enjoy the view.

In short, European train travel is a delight. If you have never experienced this mode of transportation, you are in for a treat.

TRAIN TIPS

TRAIN TICKETS

Years ago, having a root canal was less painful than trying to buy train tickets via the Internet. The purchase involved having three or more screens open on the computer so David and I could translate the site as we went along. Then, after an hour or two of frustration, we would discover that the ticket information "went through," but our US credit card was not acceptable to the foreign site. Hours of agony had gotten us closer to a nervous breakdown but no closer to taking a train in Europe!

Thankfully those days are long gone. Now it is so easy to buy train tickets online there is no excuse for not doing so.

If you can print an airline boarding pass on your computer, you can easily navigate the computer to buy train tickets. Most European rail lines now accept American credit cards so you will have no trouble buying discounted tickets in advance, and, in many cases, you can print your tickets at home just as you would print your E-ticket for an airline. Just follow the advice listed below and you'll soon be riding the rails like a pro.

Trainline.eu serves twenty countries and sells tickets for fourteen trainlines.This site is the best thing to come along for American travelers since ATM cards! It's an easy to use site in English that allows you to choose between discounted first and second class seat prices. You can choose your seat assignment and print your tickets in moments.

Pay with a credit card or PayPal and either print your E-ticket at home or print it out once you get to the station. Remember, book as early as possible to get the cheapest rate.

I have used this site and highly recommend it. I imagine Trainline.eu will meet all of your train ticket needs all over Western Europe, but I'll list three other sites in case you need to travel an obscure route or have a particularly complex itinerary.

ITALIAN TRAIN LINE

Trenitalia.com is the Italian train line, which you can use in its English version, but I highly recommend making your life as easy as possible by using italiarail.com. This site sells Trenitalia tickets that are just as cheap or cheaper than Trenitalia (cheaper especially for two or more people), lists place names in English versions

(Florence, not Firenze), accepts US credit cards and allows you to choose your seat assignment.

You will not print your ticket but will receive a PNR (passenger name record) booking code which you simply give the conductor once you're on board the train. Either that or you can collect your tickets from any self-service kiosk in the Trenitalia train station. There is a nominal fee for italiarail.com's service (€3.50 at this writing), but that is a small price to pay for all the convenience the site offers.

German Train Line

bahn.de is the German train line site. Click on "Deutschland" at the top of the page to access a drop-down menu where you can choose English as the language for the site. You might want to click "Saver Fare Finder" before entering your departure and arrival cities and dates to ensure you are given the cheapest rates.

You can use American credit cards, choose your seats, and print your tickets before leaving home for a nominal fee under €5.

Railbookers.com

Railbookers is one last idea if you want to travel several countries by rail but are wary of making all the complex arrangements. This site will make all hotel, transfer and train reservations for you. Of course this service will cost more than if you did all the work yourself, but with a particularly complicated itinerary, you may find the extra charge to be worthwhile. Also, if there is a train strike (David and I were victims of a strike in Paris, so it took us all day instead of a few hours to reach Colmar,

France.), Railbookers can help make other arrangements.

RAILROAD TIPS

The Man in Seat 61 (seat61.com) - I cannot recommend this award-winning site highly enough. The Man in Seat 61 (seat61.com) is literally jam-packed with all the information you need to make any train trip whatsoever, whether you are taking the Chunnel from London to Paris or the Trans-Siberian Railway.

While I highly recommend the Seat 61 site, I would dissuade you from using the RailEurope.com site that is located in the United States. While the United States based Rail Europe.com may seem convenient, their tickets are sometimes much more expensive because they include an extra charge for their services via the telephone, a high fee if you need tickets shipped to you, and worst of all, limited routes and no discounted prices for their rail tickets.

It is now so easy to buy rail tickets from one of the sources I mentioned earlier that there is no reason whatsoever to use Rail Europe that is based in the United States. (Note that the Rail Europe that operates out of Britain does offer discounted tickets, but this site is not available to residents buying tickets from the US.)

Also, you will probably find that a Eurail Pass is more expensive and more difficult to use than simply buying your long distance tickets in advance via the Internet.

Train Stations

In small towns there will be only one train station, but in large cities there will be many. In large cities, sometimes trains heading in certain directions leave only from particular stations; in that case, you would not have a choice but would have to leave from the station heading to your destination. If you do have a choice of stations, however, book your reservation carefully so that you depart from the station most convenient to your apartment rental. Booking sites will list all the stations in a city for you so you can make sure you are reserving a seat in the right station.

Seat Reservations

I've traveled by train quite a bit and have noticed that some countries are sticklers for rules while others have a more laid-back attitude. Out of ignorance, I once ended up in seats not assigned to me in both France and Italy. The French never questioned me, but the Italians didn't let me get away with anything. I was even charged a fine for being in the wrong car and seat altogether. All in all, I was lucky though. Since some cars regularly split off from the main train and go in a different direction, I'm glad I didn't end up going to Hamburg when I intended to go to Marseille! You will want to make sure you get the right car for this reason too.

So, to help you avoid any problems, here's the easiest way to find your coach and seat. All coaches are numbered on the coach door. Note that different numbers are assigned to first or second class (1-8 might be first class while 9-22 are second class). Look at the doors to find the number noted on your ticket and find your seat by looking at the numbers above each seat. In France, for example, there will be a billboard at the platform showing you where to stand so that you can easily find the car you need. Coaches with numbers 1-6 will be in the "A" section, numbers 7-11 in the "B" section and so on. Stand in this area of the track and search the coaches for your number when the train rolls in.

VALIDATE YOUR TICKET

If you bought your tickets on-line, you need carry only the ticket or PNR (personal name record) code you printed at home. You will show this to the ticket inspector when he makes his rounds through the coaches. But, if you bought a ticket locally, you must validate it in one of the automatic machines before you board. You'll see these machines, similar to a time clock, at every platform entrance. Simply insert the ticket, wait for the click, and take the ticket with you so you can show it later to the inspector.

LANGUAGE BARRIERS

Do not worry about language barriers in train stations as signage always includes English, and pictograms help to clarify any doubts you might have about the location of restrooms or information booths. But it is important to note that your destination may be spelled differently from what you expect. The cities Americans call Venice and Florence are Venezia and Firenze to Italians, so those are the names you'll see on the notice boards. Any time you are using trains, research the names used in the European countries before you leave home or get clarification at the information booth.

ALL STATIONS ARE NOT CREATED EQUALLY

Large stations in big cities like Paris, Florence, Madrid, and Berlin have all rail lines housed in one building. You may find thirty to forty tracks parallel to one another. Transporting your luggage is easy in these stations because everything is on one level.

Unfortunately, in small towns where there are only two or three tracks, you will probably arrive at one track, go inside the building and go down a set of stairs and then up another set of stairs to get to the tracks on the other side. Carrying your luggage up and down these stairs, which sometime amount to four sets, can be a struggle. If you didn't pack lightly, you might want to check with the inspector to see if you can arrange a porter's help. I was charged €5 for this service once, but I would have happily paid twice that to avoid what amounted to over eighty steps.

DISABILITIES

If you have a disability of any sort, whether you have a heart condition or are confined to a wheelchair, some train stations pose particular problems that can be overcome with a bit of advance planning. For example, if your heart condition prohibits you from carrying luggage up and down the many flights of stairs that a smaller train station requires, as I mentioned above, ask at the ticket booth for help. You will either be allowed to use a porter's services for a small tip, access an elevator unavailable to the general public, or be escorted across the tracks by a railroad official. For more information on disabilities involving a wheelchair, consult the excellent disabilities section on the website, seat61.com.

CARPOOLING

Did you ever carpool in college when you needed to reach your home which was several states away? In those days, you put a note on the bulletin board and crossed your fingers someone headed your way would give you a ride for the price of sharing gasoline costs. This is the business concept behind BlaBla Car and Carpooling, ride sharing services with six million members in over twenty European countries.

Let's say you're in Paris where the weather is terrible with unexpected rain and low temperatures for several days of your trip. Rather than be stuck in these miserable conditions, you decide to go to Marseille where it's sunny and warm. But it is too late to take advantage of discounted train tickets (Remember these have to be ordered 60 to 90 days in advance to get the cheapest rates.), so you decide to use BlaBlaCar.com.

Both BlaBlaCar.com and Carpooling.com work on the same principles as Uber and Lyft. You go to a site and register by entering your information and creating a profile. Interestingly, the name "BlaBla" comes from the ability to indicate how much talking you want to do during the trip so you can travel with like-minded travelers! The company decides on a fair price for sharing the gasoline costs on this city to city trip--the driver is not allowed to make a profit but the company adds a small percentage fee for making the transaction--and you decide if this is agreeable.

If all the details--the cost, date, number of stops, time of departure and arrival--are agreeable, you've got a ride! At the end of the trip, you and the driver will assign each other a rating which will become part of your respective profiles.

Remember, BlaBla and Carpooling are alternatives to the train for city to city travel, but they do not serve transportation needs within a city itself.

FOOD

Sit back for a moment and close your eyes. Think of the place you'd most like to visit in Europe. What country captured your imagination and won't let go? Or is it a city that's always tugged at your dreams? Can you see yourself walking down the quaint cobblestone street? How about sitting at a sidewalk cafe having a glass of wine?

If you can't imagine walking down that street or having that glass of wine, it's probably because your obstinate, logical brain has kicked in and told you the trip is too expensive. Even though you've already seen how you can save enormous amounts of money by finding the cheapest flight, renting an apartment, and using public transportation, your brain is still quoting travel agent prices and shaking a finger in your face, reminding you that you can't afford such extravagances.

BUT THAT PART OF YOUR BRAIN IS WRONG.

I can show you how to have the European trip you've dreamed of all your life, and it won't cost any more than a vacation at an American beach. And, no, tell that part of your brain that is screaming right now that I'm not going to suggest you do anything illegal. All I am going to ask you to do is make one small modification in only one area. That's all. You get the trip you've always dreamed of in return for one little compromise. But that compromise is essential. While you can save a lot of money with the tips you already have, this last one is the key to the cheapest European trip possible.

So, what will it be? On which item would you be willing to compromise to make your dream trip affordable?

Choose between these two things: Seeing none of the twenty or so sites on your list in the European city of your dreams or dining in restaurants.

I certainly hope you chose the second item. It would be pointless to travel several thousand miles to the place you'd been dreaming about all your life and never see any of the sites. No, the last item, eating in restaurants, is a small compromise to make considering all you get in return.

Not eating in restaurants does not mean you won't eat well. Or enjoy regional cuisine. Or ever go hungry. Or suffer in any way. What not eating in restaurants does mean is that you will be saving a huge sum of money.

Next to lodging, food costs in restaurants account for the most expensive part of a traditional trip. But, instead of spending $30-80 a day on dine-in establishments, you'll be able to eat quite well and sample all the regional cuisine for about $8-12 a day. That kind of savings makes all the difference in planning a trip you can afford.

Think about it for a minute. Twenty-somethings often travel the world for months because they can do it so cheaply. Their shoestring budgets are possible because they stay in hostels with shared bedrooms and a bathroom down the hall while they prepare their own food in the hostel kitchens.

But seeing the world the way I suggest incorporates the budgetary advantages of hostel travel with all the amenities the Baby Boomer generation desires. Tightwads travel as cheaply, or more cheaply in most cases, than footloose college students, but we travel in style, eat well, and sleep in luxurious accommodations. It is truly five-star travel on a one-star budget. You can't ask for more than that!

Please understand. I love to cook and bake at home. Every day, *The New York Times* sends me recipes from great chefs. I have a three-inch ring binder bulging with recipes I've collected online or from magazines that I have tried and found delicious. For years, I've been making all of my own bread, scones, tomato sauce, and salad dressings, and any day now I expect to master yogurt. No dessert that hasn't been made from scratch ever leaves my kitchen.

When I travel to Europe I want to experience all the gourmet treats that another cuisine has to offer, but the thought of spending hours in the kitchen after a day of museum-hopping is unappetizing. Yet, the idea of eating all my meals in restaurants is cost-prohibitive. The approach that follows is the solution to this dilemma.

People sometimes complain that cooking is not their idea of a vacation, but if you follow David's and my example, you'll find that cooking takes less time than finding a good restaurant. Our rule is that one person cooks and the other person cleans up. I don't think we've ever spent more than ten minutes either cooking or cleaning.

Actually, though, "cooking" is something of a misnomer. No one wants to prepare a Thanksgiving dinner while on vacation; besides, you'd be too tired to appreciate an elaborate dinner at the end of a long day anyway. David and I don't actually cook on vacation so much as we assemble. I'll tell you more about the "assembling" approach in a bit.

ADVANTAGES TO PREPARING YOUR OWN FOOD

I truly believe you'll find that eating in your apartment is, in the long run, not really a compromise at all. It has many advantages you haven't even realized yet. Honestly, David and I prefer to prepare our own meals, and I'll tell you exactly why.

SAMPLE THE LOCAL CUISINE

David and I aren't foodies, but, as I mentioned before, we like to eat well, and we certainly don't go to Europe to eat peanut butter and jelly sandwiches. We want to sample the local cuisine; we just don't want to pay a fortune for the privilege. That's why preparing, or, more accurately, assembling, our own food is such an advantage.

BAREFOOT BREAKFASTS AND SHOELESS SUPPERS

Because our days are jam-packed with places to see, we like leisurely mornings and lazy nights. David and I want to have breakfast in our pajamas before we shower, get dressed, and face the day. Besides, neither one of us is much good without caffeine, so that's a necessary ingredient of every successful morning. At night we like to relax after a long sightseeing day, kick off our shoes, complain about our aching feet, and have a long "happy hour" tasting some local cheeses and wines before contemplating dinner.

And that dinner is a lot easier to come by if we eat in our apartment rather than wander back outside. You might think that two people who are united in their enthusiasm for estate sales and love for all the dogs and cats in the world would be able to choose a restaurant, but that is never the case. My charming little cafes look like money pits to David, while his choices offer all the menu flexibility of uncooked pasta. Rather than wander around for hours arguing, we do much better when we stay home. Besides, just the thought of putting our shoes on again is enough to keep us rooted in place.

ICE THOSE DRINKS

Another reason I particularly like preparing our own food is because, while I consider myself European in many respects, I still cannot learn to love tepid drinks. My caffeine of choice is iced tea but it's only brown water without the ice. When we have our own kitchen, I can pop the ice cube trays (Buy these at big box stores or yard sales for pennies and leave them behind when you return home.) into the freezer and have all the ice I want.

TRY LOCAL BEER AND WINE

While I'm an iced tea connoisseur, David is a beer aficionado and likes to taste all the regional brews wherever we go. This would be beyond his budget in restaurants where a beer costs €5-8, but easily affordable in grocery stores with each beer weighing in at less than €1.

In countries famous for their wines, rather than paying €4 a glass in a restaurant, you can buy an entire bottle for that price at a grocery store.

We can have snacks, too. If we get hungry at midnight, we only have to make our way to the kitchen, not the end of the block.

EXPERIMENT A LITTLE

Have you ever ordered an expensive entree in a restaurant only to find it did not please your palate? It is so disappointing to leave a restaurant with a bad taste in your mouth and less cash in your wallet. When you use my suggestions, however, you can be a culinary explorer without so much as taking a bite out of the budget.

This is one of the advantages David and I particularly like about preparing our own food--it allows room in the budget for experimentation. We don't risk costly mistakes in restaurants but can try a small nibble of this or that from the grocery's deli case or from the local market. It's easier to buy more of what we like when we know we haven't wasted money on food we hated.

For example, using this method, we discovered in Italy, that the best ham in the world is prosciutto cotto ham, while porchetta ranks right up there with the best pork entree we've ever put in our mouths. In Florence, the Tuscan approach to cooking chicken by taking a splatch-cocked chicken and placing it directly on the grill with a brick on top yields a bit of poultry perfection!

In France, we discovered croque monsieurs, an open-faced sandwich with ham, cheese and bechamel sauce, which I'm sure I could eat happily every day for the rest of my life. We would never have tried any of these in a restaurant because we would not have wanted to spend money on something that may or may not have been a sure bet. But because we tasted a tidbit in a market or deli, we knew we'd never go wrong with those choices.

Indulge Obsessions

Buying in grocery stores also means you can indulge your obsessions. For example, I love fresh buffalo mozzarella which is a lot cheaper in markets than it is when ordered as an appetizer in a restaurant (Besides, whoever gets enough in those skimpy appetizers?) Whether your weakness is pastries, chocolates or wine, buying in grocery stores or markets rather than restaurants is the smart way to indulge.

How to Do It

Before you commit to a particular apartment, make sure the kitchen will meet your needs. Remember, you probably won't need an oven unless you're planning a special holiday dinner, but a microwave, stove top burners, toaster oven, refrigerator and freezer are essential.

The size of the kitchen is irrelevant. David and I have worked in kitchens that were as spacious as ours in Tucson, and others so tiny that only one person could be in the kitchen at a time, so don't worry about size. This is your home for a week or two, not a lifetime; you're not experimenting with gourmet recipes, so, as long as the major appliances are there, a lot of space is unnecessary.

You might ask your potential landlord if basic condiments will be at the house. Again, this is something that varies widely. Some landlords, with many bookings, will allow the previous tenant's olive oil, spices, jelly and so on to remain in the apartment while other owners clear out everything. Just to be on the safe side, we always throw a picnic-size set of salt and pepper shakers in our bags as well as artificial sweetener. If you have favorite spices you cannot live without, put a tablespoon or so of each spice in little baggies, label them, and stow them in your checked luggage.

Other items to pack, if you have room, are some plastic zip-lock bags and small rolls of plastic wrap and aluminum foil. You will also find it a cost-savings to take your own non-plastic grocery bags. European grocery stores charge for each plastic bag they supply, so taking your own cuts that cost, helps the environment and provides you with a much sturdier bag. Since you may be carrying groceries for a block rather than a few steps to the trunk of your car, you will find sturdier grocery bags helpful.

From the Grocery Store

Even though grocery store locations will probably be listed in the information provided by our landlord, David and I still ask for directions as soon as we arrive at the apartment so we can get clarification if needed. After a short nap (That's usually the only way we can deal with jet lag.), we inventory the kitchen to see if anything has been left behind, make a list, and head out for the store.

Grocery stores in Europe are just like your hometown stores with only a few exceptions. Europeans have a clever way to ensure carts are returned to the proper place. When you are getting a cart, you will find them chained together. You must insert a euro in the little locking device on the cart handle which is returned to you when you return the cart.

In the store itself, there's only one thing to remember. When buying produce you must weigh the produce, choose the correct pictogram from the chart to identify your selection, and attach the price tag to the item or bag.

At check-out, the last difference you'll notice is that the clerks do not pack your bags for you. You are expected to do that yourself using the bags you so cleverly brought from home.

David and I have spent some interesting moments and had some fascinating conversations in grocery stores all over the world, trying to figure out what butter or cream or jelly is called. We've found most people will go out of their way to help us, the pictures on the products themselves help a great deal, Google's translate app aids in label deciphering, and, if all else fails and we buy the wrong thing, we figure it's part of the learning experience and not a costly mistake Usually we get our bearings quickly, and, since we use the same store for a few visits, we quickly learn where to find what we need.

On our list are the basics that usually include: eggs (There will be several kinds of eggs depending on what feed the chickens were given.), butter (Look in the deli case for locally fresh-churned butter. European butter is the best in the world because the fat content is so high.), bag lettuce that's been pre-washed, oil and vinegar or salad dressing, cream for David's coffee (He always takes his own coffee plus a simple little one-cup cone drip coffee maker.), sugar for my tea (I always take my own tea bags and artificial sweetener), vegetables, fruits, sodas, beer, wine, bread (We like fresh loaves from the bakery section.), jelly, cheese, deli cold cuts (Whatever looks good in the case. This is where it's fun to experiment.), paper towels (We use towels for napkins, too, although it's easy enough to carry a few cloth napkins since you can wash them when you do your regular laundry. By the way, if you're in a restaurant, remember to call "napkins" by their European name, "serviettes." Otherwise, the wait staff will assume you're asking for a woman's sanitary product!)

We also like to shop local outdoor markets. That is where we discovered porchetta in the market next to our apartment building near Rome and some flavorful goat cheese in France. Besides finding culinary treats that you know are fresh-that-morning off the farm, you can practice your language skills and enjoy interacting with the locals.

From Local Bakeries and Delis

Once you've stocked up on the basics, you can indulge in the pleasures to be found in European bakeries and delis. Getting takeaway, as it's called, is very different in Europe, and you will be pleased with what you discover.

In the United States we are accustomed to fast-food takeout that tastes only tolerable and is loaded with calories, fat, and cholesterol. This is not the case in Europe. They have few hamburger or fast-food chains as most of their delis are small family-owned places that have been in business, in the same location, for generations. The chefs preparing the food displayed in the store are often just as well-trained as the chefs working in expensive restaurants. That is why many of these places are as famous as some popular restaurants and are listed in guidebooks along with those much more expensive restaurants.

You'll know that the food you find here is fresh. It was prepared that day because delis don't have enough space to store leftovers. The food will also taste delicious because it contains no additives--most are prohibited by law, unlike the States--and no extra sugar or salt. GMO foods and antibiotics are outlawed in Europe, so you do not need to worry about those issues either. Truly, if you've never tried takeaway in Europe you are in for a culinary treat!

Some delis have windows opening on the street so you can stand on the sidewalk and place your order while others require you to go inside to make your request at the counter. You will also find sit-down restaurants that allow takeaway. You will soon find your favorite places and learn to get there before the crowds.

Don't forget dessert. Truly, I've always thought simply looking at the offerings in European pastry shops was akin to enjoying paintings in a museum; their edible art is a joy to see as well as to eat. So ignore any guilty feelings you might have and sample all that look delicious. After all, indulging in these treats is one of the reasons you came to Europe. Besides, you will undoubtedly lose weight because you'll do so much more walking. I always lose eight to twelve pounds in Europe.

ASSEMBLING NOT COOKING

In the time it would take a non-savvy tourist couple to get dressed, agree on a restaurant, find the restaurant and place their order, you can assemble dinner, eat in a leisurely fashion with your shoes off, clean up, and be sitting on the terrace enjoying the sunset and a glass of wine long before that other couple even gets served. And you will pay under €10 for a sumptuous meal for two instead of €80 for a restaurant dinner that may or may not have been enjoyable. While I'd like to believe all restaurant food is delicious, I have too often been disappointed. I have also found that there is sometimes no correlation between price and quality. Some of the most expensive dinners I've ever ordered have been among the worst.

The secret to easy dinner preparation is assembling, not cooking. Your main dish is from a bakery, restaurant, or carryout shop, and you simply augment that with the freshly baked bread and salad greens you bought at the grocery store. Add a pastry for dessert, some local wines or beer, and you'd be hard-pressed to think anyone was eating any better than you.

The beauty of preparing meals this way is that the delicious entree, a reflection of regional cuisine, has been professionally prepared with local ingredients, but it will cost a pittance of what you would pay in a restaurant for the exact same thing. And it will take less time to heat your entree than it did to choose it from all the delectable offerings in the deli!

Truly, with the assembling approach, it's a very simple matter to add just a couple other items to your deli entree to create a delicious dinner.

Remember, by traveling the Tightwad Way you are eating well, experiencing the best of the local cuisine, and not spending hours or a small fortune per day to do it. You're not missing out on anything. In fact, you'll be feeling smug while you pity that non-savvy tourist couple waiting for their dinner in a restaurant!

Breakfast doesn't require any more effort than dinner. It's certainly not difficult to prepare a couple eggs, toast some bakery bread, peel a banana, and pour some orange juice.

For lunch, you can do one of two things depending on where you are. If you're in a large city, it's easier and faster to simply get a carryout item from a local shop. Look for long lines because that's where you'll find the best food. This is also a good time to re-fill your water bottle.

If you're driving in the countryside, pack a simple lunch of deli meat sandwiches and some fresh fruit before you leave your apartment. For all the reasons I mentioned before, those deli sandwiches you prepare using the best deli ingredients and the freshest bakery bread will not disappoint. Rather than searching for a restaurant in a small town, you can find a shady spot under a tree and have a picnic.

Remember that a small collapsible cooler comes in very handy if you're going to be using a car during your trip, so don't forget to pack it before leaving home.

SAMPLE MENUS

To show you how easy this is, here are a couple sample menus that David and I have used recently.

DAY ONE -

Breakfast - Scrambled eggs with bits of prosciutto and cheese, croissant with freshly-churned butter and strawberry jam, banana, coffee and iced tea.

Lunch - Deli cold cuts sandwiches, on slices of bakery bread, tomatoes and cheese. Carrot slices and potato chips. Water from our water bottles.

Dinner - Huge triangle of pizza rustica (As thick as quiche and even more delicious.), salad greens with fresh tomatoes, fresh bread with freshly-churned butter, wine, and beer. Cannoli (pastry shell filled with sweetened ricotta cheese) for dessert.

DAY TWO -

Breakfast - Fried eggs, bread with freshly-churned butter and strawberry jam, orange slices, coffee and iced tea.

Lunch - Because it's a "city" day, we find a little deli

where we buy a couple slices of pizza. David and I sit on a bench to eat and watch the people pass by.

Dinner - Lasagna from the incredible takeout restaurant across the street from our apartment, fresh bread with freshly-churned butter, salad greens, wine and beer. We decide to go to Toni's, our favorite little gelato place down the street, for a cup of icy cold dessert.

Just writing these words has made me hungry, and I can't tell you what I'd give right now for either a slice of pizza rustica or a serving of Frontoni's lasagna. It always seems to me that most anything David and I buy from these small, individually owned bakeries/restaurants is so well-prepared, with the freshest ingredients, that it always tastes delicious. I honestly cannot think of a time we've been disappointed with an entree. The only problem I have is that I become addicted to something I find particularly great, like the lasagna from the place across from our Rome apartment, and never want to try anything else. Out of our seven nights in Rome, I think we had lasagna four times!

I hope I've convinced you that you are sacrificing nothing when you eat the Tightwad Way except the nuisance of searching for restaurants. By shopping the local grocery stores and markets, you will interact with locals, learn more about the culture and the language, enjoy the country's unique cuisine, and save hundreds of dollars. Living well is an art form in Europe, and you will be doing just that by shopping and dining as Europeans do.

BENDING THE BUDGET WITHOUT BREAKING IT

In the beginning of this book I said I had more wanderlust than money, and that is still true today. But now that I know how to plan a vacation to Europe that costs no more than a trip to Miami Beach, I am confident my wanderlust will eventually be sated. It may take another twenty years to reach every far-flung corner, but the skills and money-saving tips in this book will eventually take me to every place I want to see.

I hope you now feel the same. Travel does not have to be an expensive luxury. I believe travel can, and should be, one of life's necessities. Just as you plan for mortgage payments or car insurance, why not include European travel in your budget?

With a little patience, a bit of saving, and the implementation of the suggestions in this book, you'll soon be exploring Europe and reaping the many rewards of a well-traveled life.

WHAT ABOUT SOLO TRAVELERS

In the beginning of this book, I promised that two people traveling together could have a wonderful travel experience with luxurious accommodations, excellent dining, and sightseeing galore for less than $98 a day per person, but if you're a solo traveler, you may be wondering if it would cost you a great deal more. After all, don't organized tours usually charge a hefty "single supplement"?

Although I did it twenty years ago, I'm delighted to tell you that a solo traveler can still travel even more cheaply than a couple because I did just that during the month of June, 2016. While David stayed home caring for our furry children, I lived in Florence, Italy, for a month while taking a class on Renaissance art at the British Institute of Florence. My well-located one-bedroom apartment, all my food (I found an excellent restaurant-deli where I bought several entrees at a time, although I also joined friends for an occasional happy hour buffet.), transportation, museum admissions and course fees averaged $88 a day!

So, whether you are single or traveling with another, it is easy to plan a wonderful trip that will enrich your life without bankrupting your budget. All it takes is a bit of planning and a willingness to follow the suggestions in this book.

Part Three

Practical Advice

While the first part of this book covered the important steps involved in planning a frugal trip, be sure to check this section for tips that will help you get the most from your European adventures. Here you will find practical advice about everything from toilets to tulips. Chances are good, too, that there might be a personal anecdote previously published on my blog that will help illustrate a point or help you avoid one of the costly mistakes I made.

Is Travel Medical Insurance Necessary

Only you can answer this question because it depends on your risk tolerance. In an article by Robert Firpo-Cappiello, the editor in chief of *Budget Travel* said this in a November, 2016, blog post.

In general, Budget Travel does not recommend travel insurance. Instead, before you travel, check all your existing insurance policies to make sure you'll be covered wherever you'll be traveling—including health, auto, and any possessions (which are sometimes covered by home insurance). That said, if you're booking a package tour or cruise make sure you understand the cancellation policy and consider paying a small premium if you think there's a chance you'll cancel.

-Robert Firpo-Cappiello

I never buy trip insurance but many people never leave home without it. If you do not have insurance that is applicable everywhere in the world (Medicare is not.) or if you have chronic health issues, you may want to consider travel insurance. While I am not endorsing any company, these names are frequently recommended in travel forums as places to learn about travel insurance options: Squaremouth.com and InsureMyTrip.com.

Here are the reasons I do not purchase insurance. If I have to cancel or re-book a trip, the penalties charged by airlines and apartment owners are less than the cost of trip insurance. Since I don't purchase train tickets or museum passes until 90 days or a month before I leave, I am fairly confident at that point that the trip will take place. Again, if I must cancel, these tickets will be far less than the cost of insurance

I always take the precaution of asking my doctor for an antibiotic, such as a "Z-Pack," before I leave home. While I only had to use the pack once when I contracted what felt like bronchitis in Nice, France, this $10 "insurance" investment is worth it for peace of mind.

For any other medical problem, I have found European pharmacists to be extremely helpful. Unlike their American counterparts, these pharmacists can make diagnoses and prescribe over-the-counter drugs that will cure most of the minor problems that can arise on a trip. Never hesitate to ask a European pharmacist for advice. Almost all of them speak English and you'll be amazed at the amount of time and attention they will devote to your problem.

If a more serious issue arises, these countries where universal health care is the norm, rarely charge more than nominal fees. When my friend broke her leg in Provence, France, Dr. Vladimir Pop, who spoke perfect English at the Joan of Arc Clinic in Arles, took x-rays and set her leg with a temporary cast (All that was appropriate at that point.) for $75. She was also given a "prescription" for a wheelchair, which another friend and I were able to pick up for her at another clinic, free of charge.

We are accustomed in the United States to paying huge bills for injuries. All of us have heard horror stories of people who were bankrupted by one serious accident, but this simply is not the case abroad. I have heard over and over again of people who had a heart attack or broke a wrist in Europe and were either charged nothing at all or given a modest bill. Truly, the cost of travel insurance is far higher than most any medical fee you'd pay in Europe.

But what if the very worst happens and your husband or wife dies while on vacation? Travel experts generally agree that the best decision in this frightening scenario is to seek help from your consulate or embassy representative who will arrange cremation, if that is what you desire. It is then easy to transport the remains back to a final resting place in the States.

How to Get Free Pet-Sitting

Nothing will destroy your carefully orchestrated budget of $98 a day faster than having to pay $35-50 a day for a kennel. If you don't have a friend, neighbor, or relative who can temporarily adopt your furry child, you may hire someone to come over every day to feed your cat or walk your dog. The only problem with that idea is, if you have a shy cat like our Guido, he will hide every time the caregiver shows up and nearly perish from lack of attention.

When we returned from a month in Mexico, Guido sat on the steps meowing for the next eight hours until he had no voice left. He might have been telling us the news, but we think it more likely he was giving us a piece of his mind for having been gone so long.

Rather than have that ever happen again, we found a solution that has solved the cat and dog problem for the past nine years.

When it was impossible for friends to sit for us any longer, I remembered a National Public Radio interview I'd heard a few years ago about a company called House Carers.com. The website unites pet sitters with vacationers for a match that benefits both; the pet sitter gets a free vacation and the pet owner gets free pet care.

I wrote a description of our house, our pets, and a few other details and placed an ad for free (home owners pay no fee while would-be pet/house sitters pay $50 or so for twelve months). Within five days we had 45 applicants!

We emailed a number of delightful people, checked a lot of references, and finally decided on a retired couple we thought would be perfect for our situation. They were anxious to explore a different part of the country, and we were delighted to have loving people care for our four-footed family members. And the price was right for all of us. They got a free vacation and we got free pet care!

Helpful Hints for Using House Carers

House Carers has lots of information on its site to help you place a homeowner ad.

Do a search yourself, for free, to get a feel for the kind of ad you think will be successful.

When writing your copy, keep in mind that the applicant will want to know details about your house (number of bedrooms, bath, garden), what attractions are near your home, and what his responsibilities will be in regards to your home (gardening, lawn mowing?) and pets (Are pets on special diets or medications?).

Do not hesitate to ask for and to check references. After all, you're entrusting your house and beloved pets to this person. You have a right to know she is reliable and honest.

While we know the people who sit for us, usually retired couples, are honest and reliable because their references told us so, we also take the precaution of putting a few of our cherished or irreplaceable items in the trunk of the car or in a locked closet. But, in nine years of using sitters several times a year, we have never had anything stolen. One couple accidentally broke a bowl and tried to pay us for it. Another time, a sitter broke a pair of scissors and replaced them with a better pair.

We have also found that the sitters, because of the

trust we place in them, return that trust and end up becoming friends. We still, to this day, exchange emails with our very first sitters from nine years ago, and we would be happy to have any of our sitters visit us at any time!

I don't know how many responses most people receive, but I would guess more desirable locations probably get more than most. Still, even though the time required to find the right sitter may vary, no matter where you live there is probably someone who would be willing to care for your house and pets while you're away.

SAMPLE LETTER FOR REQUESTING SITTERS

Here is the letter we used nine years ago when we lived in San Diego. We use a variation of this now that we live in Tucson.

We live in a very comfortable two story house (two bedrooms--a California king bed and a queen--and study, one and a half baths, with enclosed private terraces front and back) in the charming beach town of Encinitas in San Diego North County, just a 25-minute drive north of the city of San Diego.

We are three miles from the ocean, 25 minutes from San Diego's many attractions, 45 minutes from Mexico, and about an hour's drive from Los Angeles. There are enough day-trip attractions to keep anyone happy for months, and Encinitas itself is a delight! A car is necessary, but a light rail line connects the coast from Tijuana, Mexico to Los Angeles. The station is in downtown Encinitas.

Our indoor-only cat is easy to care for and will perform somersaults for you after you become friends. Our dog is incredibly smart, seemingly a human-with-fur, who requires a couple visits to the outdoors each day and one walk around the block every evening. Both pets are mature and very easy care.

We are looking for a mature pet sitter with many references who truly loves animals. It is also important to us that our house be well-cared for; we don't expect you to do spring cleaning while you're here, but it would be nice if the house were as clean when we return as it is when we leave.

Thank you for considering us. We live in one of the most desirable areas of the United States and think our townhome is an ideal vacation spot! If you would like to visit this part of the country and love animals, please let us know.

We ask the sitters to arrive the day before we leave, staying in our guest room overnight, so we can go over details with them. We try to put everyone at ease by walking them through the house, answering any questions they have, and recommending they consult a three-ring binder which contains Helpful Hints about taking care of the animals and the house along with copies of all the instruction manuals for the appliances. We include emergency information for our pets along with phone numbers of plumbers and electricians we've used in the past.

We also include local restaurant suggestions along with some ideas about day trips. Any maps or spare restaurant menus we can find are also included. Before leaving, we try to introduce our wonderful neighbors to the sitters so the sitters feel they will be able to identify a friendly face in the neighborhood.

Another nice idea is to either treat your sitters to dinner, leave them a gift coupon for a local eatery or bakery, or bring them a special souvenir from your travels.

OTHER HOUSE-SITTING SITES

Should House Carers not meet your needs, you might try one of these other pet-sitting sites: MindMyHouse. com and Luxury House Sitting.com

RESOURCES - GATHERING THE INFORMATION YOU NEED

FOR INSPIRATION

"Vagabonding involves taking an extended time-out from your normal life—six weeks, four months, two years—to travel the world on your own terms." That's what Rolf Potts advocates in his book about travel. He believes Americans are so consumed with achieving the American Dream, so caught up with mortgages and monthly payments and all the things advertisers lead them to believe they need, that they limit travel to "short, frenzied bursts." Their travel, packaged as vacations, simply become another item to purchase each year and schedule for one or two weeks between May and September. In contrast, Potts would like us to become explorers and discover our world during long, leisurely trips where we see a lot—but experience even more.

Potts's excellent blog contains more travel information than you're likely to find at your local library. Vagablogging also features guest writers who are busily writing about the world they are idly exploring. Don't miss this treasure trove of information.

For Cultural Appreciation

Read, see, and learn as much as you can about the places you'll be visiting. Study the history, read about the artists, and see movies set in the country where you'll be staying. All of this will provide a background to help you appreciate the country's cultural riches and enhance your pleasure in "seeing the real thing" when you're there in person. Find annotated reading lists, movie suggestions, and historical information on the Internet or in guidebooks.

How to get the trip information you need

Slow Travel

David and I, using our separate computers, comb the Internet for information when we're preparing for a trip, but the source we return to again and again is Slow Travel.com. Here, travelers like us who eschew tours in favor of staying in one place for a week or so to wander leisurely, post their reviews about everything you can imagine. You will find information about how to operate European appliances, where to find the best source for museum tickets, and how to navigate foreign airports so you can find the elusive hotel shuttle. There are many categories of articles to consult as well as a forum area where you can post a question.

FORUMS

Other Internet forums to check for valuable information are Frommer's and Fodor's. If you've got a question about something, chances are someone else has wondered about it, too. Find the answer in the forums.

GUIDEBOOKS

Guidebooks are such a valuable commodity you will even find uses for old ones. Buy them at yard sales or used book stores for a quarter. Outdated guides are still helpful because the four-hundred-year-old sites you want to visit haven't changed much. When you've only spent pennies on a guidebook, you won't mind ripping out pages from several books. Organize these pages into one notebook to create your own personalized guidebook that will weigh far less than most novels.

That three-ring notebook will also hold information you'll gather from the Internet. While your just-purchased, current guidebook has up-to-the-minute information about hours of operation, costs, walking tours and itineraries and your torn-apart, old guidebooks supply historical details about the sites you'll see, websites can often supply esoteric information that is not available anywhere else.

For example, David and I were uncertain about finding the shuttle to our airport hotel in Paris on the last day. We found the information we needed on a Trip Advisor page. (We still got lost, but at least we didn't get lost quite as badly as we could have!) A *New York Times* article introduced us to macaroons. (Though it would have been better for my waistline if macaroons and I had never met!) So, don't overlook the Internet as a great source of information.

BLOGS

And, of course, you do not want to forget the information available on blogs. Type two words – the destination name and the word "blog" -- in any search engine, and you will discover scads of sites where people share their travel secrets with you. This is where you'll hear about the fabulous, tucked-away-in-a-back-alley deli where the food is divine and the bill negligible, or where you'll get tips on how to avoid the latest tourist scam. The information on blogs is invaluable; no matter where you're going, somebody's already been there and would love to give you a tip or two. Scour the site, follow the links, and take notes. Write a comment on the blog or ask a question. Most blog writers are anxious to share their knowledge and will enjoy re-living their trip while helping you at the same time.

ITINERARY PLANNING

One of the most tedious aspects of planning a trip is mapping the itinerary. David and I usually have a dozen guidebooks, along with detailed notes, scattered throughout the house which we use to make sure we choose all the sites we're anxious to see along with their addresses, hours of operation, and cost. Then we plot a daily travel plan that can be accomplished by either walking or public transportation.

At least that was our approach before we discovered a wonderful free website, plnnr.com. This site helped us plan many trips in about five minutes. Unfortunately, as of this writing, the user-friendly site has been bought by the Travel Channel and is undergoing an overhaul. When it does become available again, it will make travel planning a snap. The site takes you through several steps to arrive at a detailed daily itinerary complete with maps.

It is amazingly easy to use and is like having your own personal travel agent at your command. Be on the lookout for its rebirth!

For a Remarkable Experience

Another planning site from the short-term rental folks at Airbnb is called AirbnbTrips.com. It launched in November, 2016, and aims to provide the traveler with a great deal more than just a place to lay his weary head. Everyone knows that visiting a new city where a trusted friend shows you around, introduces you to the best museums, and snags tickets for an unpublicized performance is the best way to travel, so Trips is trying to replicate that "trusted friend" experience with this new site.

In addition to renting you an apartment, you can also purchase a wide variety of experiences on the Airbnb site that you would not ordinarily discover on your own. For example, if you're going to be in Los Angeles on Valentine's Day and need a romantic venue, you might purchase a four-course dinner by a famous chef followed by a musical performance in a small concert hall for $175 per person. If you're heading to Cuba, take salsa and rumba lessons for three days for $95. Are you in London with sartorial questions? Spend three days with a fashion guru exploring vintage stores, eclectic shops and exhibits that will teach you all you need to know about fashion for $230.

With selections covering every imaginable experience--from pizza to prisons (Visit Nelson Mandela's cell for $299 with one of his guards.) and sports to social justice--ranging in price from reasonable to splurge, you just might find a special experience that will enhance your trip in ways you never imagined.

You can learn while traveling. There are many courses one can take all over Europe that will teach you all about country cottages in England, French cooking in Paris, tapas preparation in Spain, and art in Italy to name only a few. Check the Trip Advisor website for classes offered at your destination or any guidebook on the region you plan to visit.

One program I can highly recommend is the British Institute of Florence which is housed in Florence, Italy, the birthplace of the Renaissance. Here, classes in English teach people of all ages the Italian language or Renaissance art or drawing from some of the best teachers in the world.

I participated in a month-long High Renaissance Art class in the summer of 2016, and thought it one of the best experiences of my life. It was also one of the most economical, costing far, far less than most comparable programs. For more information, see the "monthly courses" listed under the "history of art" menu on the left side of the British Institute of Florence website. For a recounting of my daily experiences living and learning in Florence, see my blog, tightwadtravel.blogspot.com.,

NEVER TRAVEL ON A SUNDAY

As you are planning your itinerary, you'll find it helpful to remember that Sundays are reserved for families in Europe and most businesses are closed. It is wise not to plan any travel on that day because most car rental firms and many restaurants are not open for business. It's also best to plan grocery shopping earlier in the weekend.

ATTENTION ANGLOPHILES

Want to experience the London Eye—one of the tallest Ferris wheels in the world--without leaving the ground? Britain's national tourism agency's website will let you do that—and a whole lot more. There's no need to mind-the-gap here, because there is no gap. I cannot imagine a question that could not be answered by this site. The plethora of information will satisfy the most curious Anglophile. Just enter "visitbritain.us" in your search engine.

As well as the usual information provided by tourist agencies, the "About Britain" section provides details about money, medicine, time zones, the weather (The site insists it does not rain every day.), and hosts the "Image and Sound Gallery" where you can experience the London Eye or the changing of the guards at Buckingham Palace, along with a dozen or so other videos.

On the "Things to Do" page, activities to suit travelers of any age or interest are listed. In addition to walking and car itineraries—complete with maps—this section offers eight other options catering to such diverse tastes as sports, gardens, spas, shopping and cycling.

I'm particularly fond of the accommodation section

because there are self-catering rental options in "royal places" and "pubs and inns."

After you've perused the valuable information, studied the suggested activities, and plotted your visit, you can buy whatever you need—from the Oyster Card for public transportation to the London Sightseeing Pass—on the site.

But if you're still pondering the possibilities and want more information, or, perhaps, a more personal point of view, go to the excellent site beenthere-donethat.org.uk The mission of this unofficial guide to England, Scotland and Wales, is to provide, "An illustrated travel guide to Great Britain, based on personal experience of the locations, with pictures of mountains, moorlands, quaint villages, pastoral landscapes, historic buildings over 1000 years old, the coast, steam railways, flowers, fossils and much more."

There's a forum where you can pose your questions, accommodation reviews based on the authors' personal experiences, and a blog where various aspects of Britain are discussed. Be sure to click on "Links" for a thorough list of accommodations, pub guides, maps and several more noteworthy references.

LANGUAGE HELP

You'll get more smiles from the people you meet if you can speak even a few words of their language. At a minimum, it is helpful to know how to say "please," "thank you," and "Where is the toilet?" A great source of information is Fodor's Language for Travelers.com On this Internet site, you will find more than 150 words and phrases in six different categories (greetings, directions, shopping, numbers, dining out, basic phrases) for seven different languages. Another page with basic grammar and pronunciation rules will help you say words correctly. I studied Italian for a month before spending five weeks in Florence and found I could communicate fairly well.

Do not forget to download translate.google.com to your cell phone. It works offline and is invaluable for finding the word you need in a foreign language. You can also use your phone's camera to "look at" a sign or label and instantly translate it into English.

While it is helpful to learn some essential words and phrases to ease social interactions, do not worry about your lack of fluency in a foreign language. As I mentioned earlier, English is the world's universal language and you will find signage in English in all airports, train terminals, and bus stations. Also, English is the secondary language taught in all schools, so most Europeans know basic words in English even if they're not fully conversant. If you ask politely and smile, you will always find someone who will help you with any language barriers. Never let lack of knowledge of a foreign language keep you from traveling.

PACKING OVERVIEW

When I'm getting ready for a trip to Europe, I never forget what to pack as long as I've got it on a list. But keeping track of the scribbled lists is another problem altogether. One list is on my desk, another flutters on the refrigerator door, a third sits on my dresser and one is taped to the bathroom mirror. By the time I get around to packing, the barely legible lists have suffered their share of abuse, and it's a wonder I pack the map instead of the mop.

My life has gotten easier since I've discovered a site that makes list-making a snap. I can modify a generic list so that it will meet my needs whether I am going for a one-week or one-month trip. When I print the finished product, I have a legible, organized, comprehensive list of everything I need. You may find that packwhiz.com will be a great help to you, too. It just may be the next best thing to having a professional pack for you!

PACKING TIPS

Make copies of all your documents, passport, credit cards and medicine list. If you're traveling with another person, you carry his while he carries your copy. If you're traveling alone, be sure to keep this information in your carryon. That way, if the worst happens, you can survive the emergency.

Instead of carrying bulky bottles of pills, ask the pharmacist to give you flat packs that will easily fit in your carryon. That way you will have your prescription information on the package which is required by the TSA.

Don't invite thieves into your home by putting your home address on a luggage tag. Your name, cell phone, and email address are all that's needed.

Pack sanitary wipes

Travelers don't succumb to viruses because of airplane air but because of germ-laden seatback trays. You may feel like Felix Unger from *The Odd Couple* as you wipe down your tray, but that's better than spending your vacation sick in bed.

Essentials to Pack

European Night Lights

David and I are blind without our glasses or contacts. Since USA night lights won't work in European apartments, we came up with another idea. Rather than stumble around a dark apartment at night, we use small three-inch-long flashlights to find our way if we must get up. The tiny flashlights take up little suitcase space, yet they provide just enough light to find the bathroom without awakening a sleeping partner.

For Liquids

With the airlines' stringent weight restrictions, it's expensive to tote your economy-sized bottles of toiletries. Besides, it's impractical to carry them even if you use a zippered plastic bag to hold the bottles. When you unpack, you find half the liquid puddled at the bottom of the bag. Nalgene bottles are too expensive for a Tightwad Traveler, and cheap containers from super-stores leak.

So here's a suggestion for a fool-proof, leak-proof alternative. Use liquid prescription containers available at any pharmacy. The next time you pick up a prescription, ask for a few bottles in various sizes. I always offer to pay, but so far no one has allowed me to do so; I've gotten eight bottles for free at a couple different drugstores. They come in all sizes, from three to sixteen ounces. Use a permanent marker to write the contents on the bottle itself. When you need to change the contents, use fingernail polish remover to erase the old pen marker label for the new identification.

I've road-tested these and guarantee you will love them. These plastic pharmacy bottles have traveled the globe with me and not a single container has ever leaked!

LAUNDRY SOAP

The washing machine in your apartment will be smaller than the one you have back home, but still a whole lot larger than the kitchen sink. While you might want to wash one or two items in the sink using dish detergent (It works fine!), you'll need laundry detergent for those larger loads.

Rather than carry liquid that might leak or powder that adds too much weight, use an all-in-one detergent and clothes softener sheet. Cut in half, the sheet provides the right amount of suds to clean your clothes, yet it takes next to no space in your suitcase. (As of this writing, Purex is the only detergent I know of that is in sheet form, but perhaps another brand is available in your area.)

WASHCLOTHS

Most accommodations outside the United States do not supply washcloths. I carry a nylon "scrubby" for use in the shower, but I've found that carrying my own washcloth, in a zippered plastic bag, is essential for washing my face.

STAY HYDRATED

Pack an empty water bottle in your carry-on. When you've cleared security, fill your bottle at an airport drinking fountain. You won't have to wait for the flight attendant to serve you and you'll stay hydrated despite the dry atmosphere of the cabin.

When you reach your destination, your bottle can be refilled daily to serve as your daily take-along water supply.

SINK STOPPER

Many budget accommodations are lacking a sink stopper in the bathroom washbasin. Losing a contact lens down the drain will ruin your vacation, so carry a flat plastic one-size-fits-all sink stopper available for a dollar at any variety or hardware store.

ICE CUBE TRAYS

As I mentioned earlier, my morning beverage of choice is iced tea, but ice is difficult to come by in Europe. So, since iced tea is just brown water without the ice, I make my own. I buy plastic ice cube trays at a store or yard sale which take little space in my suitcase since the trays nest together. This way I enjoy cold drinks during my vacation, but, because the trays are so inexpensive, I don't worry about packing them for the return trip home. I like to leave them behind for the next iced tea drinker who might happen by.

Essential Organizational Items

Take a small roll of tape to repair maps; our wonderful Paris city map was torn in three places after only a few days.

One of those tiny staplers is also helpful because you can use it to attach receipts to brochures and organize papers.

Consider a small, 5X7 inch, note pad to use for a few important purposes. In cities, your Metro route can be recorded on a sheet each night so you don't have to re-think your connections. Having a paper with the Metro stops clearly defined is especially helpful at the end of a long, tiring day. In the country, use the tablet to record your driving route each day. You'll still consult maps, but it is easier to find your way with a tentative route in hand. The pad also comes in handy to list items needed from the grocery store or market.

Print a blank calendar from the Internet and use it to plan your itinerary before leaving home. At your European apartment, use magnets (You did remember the magnets, right?) to mount the calendar to the front of your refrigerator. Those magnets also come in handy for mounting the shopping list to the fridge, too.

Postcards or Notecards

As I mentioned earlier, if the apartment was everything you hoped it would be and the owners were accommodating in giving you lots of information about the area, you may want to leave a brief thank you note for them. I always take some postcards of my hometown, and say something like, "This apartment wasn't in Tucson but you made it feel just like home!" Also, if the owners have a guestbook, do them a favor and write a comment or two.

NEVER STAND IN LINE

There is no point wasting your time standing in two or three-hour lines, often in ninety-degree heat, to buy attraction tickets. Although organized tour companies would prefer you not know this, ALL tickets to museums and cultural sites can be purchased online before you leave home. This is what organized tour companies do, and so can you! There is usually a small fee (typically under $5) for the service, but that's a tiny price to pay for the enormous convenience of skipping the line.

Because these sites are accessed by people all over the world, the sites are easy to use and accept all US credit cards, but do make sure you use a credit card that charges no foreign transaction fee. You'll find it's a simple matter to print the ticket on your home computer.

Here are a few of the most popular attractions with the websites you need.

FOR ITALY
FLORENCE--THE FIRENZECARD.IT.

Rome, the Vatican, and Venice--The tickitalywebsite sells tickets for all these place. This is where you will find tickets for the Roman Colosseum (the regular tour as well as the newest one of the dungeons and third level), the Vatican, and the Doges Palace in Venice. Simply put tickitaly and whatever site you want (example--tickitaly Vatican) to generate the appropriate ticket-buying site.

For France

The parismuseumpass sells tickets to most of the museums in Paris, but the Louvre requires a separate ticket which can be purchased at louvre.fr/en/buy-tickets The lines at the Eiffel Tower are particularly long, so it's helpful to have an advance ticket which you can purchase here ticket.toureiffel.fr/?langue=en

For Spain

Tickets for the Alhambra and Generalife Gardens can be purchased at ticketmaster. Type "ticketmaster Alhambra tickets" in the search line.

For the Netherlands

Amsterdam's Anne Frank House sells tickets online two months prior to your visit. Go to the annefrank.org site and follow the link to buy tickets.

For any museum or site not mentioned here, simply enter the name of the attraction, along with the words "advance tickets," in your browser and you will be guided to the correct website. Note that you will often be asked to sign up, enroll, or sign in on a purchasing site, but do not worry about that. Unless you're going to be using the site to purchase many tickets over a long period, there's no need to enroll. You can buy tickets as a guest.

Free City Tours

There is never a need to pay for a tour of a city because free tours abound all over the globe. Excellent tours, often narrated by college students, are offered by Sandeman's New Europe for eighteen European cities. These are "free" in the sense that there is no up front cost, but you are expected to tip the guide, often that struggling college student, about €5 per person. If Sandeman's doesn't offer a tour where you are, you will undoubtedly find a free tour at one of these sites. freecitytour.com or thepriceoftravel.com website which lists too many free tours to count in every place from Amsterdam to Zurich!

If you prefer to move at your own pace, there are many free apps that can be downloaded onto your phone. Then all you need do is plug in your earphones, tuck your smartphone in your bag, and go! Here are a few apps to consider: Rick Steves' audio Europe walking tours and radio interviews are free and comprehensive. Steves will take you on a walking tour that will rival a pricey guided one. Or, if you prefer to be more spontaneous, try the Field Trip app which runs on your phone in the back-ground and pipes up when you come across something interesting. Still another free app to try in places of archi-tectural interest is geo tourist. You must enroll online and then the app will download to your phone.

Here's an account of the Sandeman tour David and I took in Paris.

If you wear your sturdiest walking shoes and prepare yourself for a pace more suitable for twenty-year-olds than fifty-somethings, you'll love the New Paris free walking tour.

We began at the fountain in the square called Place St. Michel and ended four hours later (with a half hour for lunch) near the Arc de Triomphe. Along the way, we learned that the Latin Quarter is named for the language spoken long ago by the scholars who studied in the area.

(Since the Sorbonne is now located there, the area is still a gathering spot for intellectuals and artists, but everyone has pretty much given up on speaking Latin!) We discovered that the flying buttresses of Notre Dame are what help support its astonishing stained glass windows; the tuileries means tile in French, so the Tuilerie Gardens pay homage to the tile works that once stood on those grounds; and that Napoleon so loved oranges that he had a huge greenhouse built to shelter orange trees, and that greenhouse has been converted into the Musee de l'Orangerie.

There were many other facts and stories Sam told during our delightful tour, but the only detail she omitted was the one I now need most. How do I cope with my aching feet?

PARTICIPATE

If you're invited to participate in a festive event, whether it is a town celebration, a family party, or a wedding, by all means do so. There's no better way to appreciate a culture than by being part of one of its celebrations.

SENIOR DISCOUNTS

Don't forget to ask for senior discounts if you are over 55 years of age; many countries offer lower admission costs and transportation discounts.

SPECIAL EVENTS

A free Internet site, eventful.com is a worldwide events guide that will help you find just about any festival, musical event, market, or art gallery that will be holding a special event when you are in town.

TOILETS NOT RESTROOMS

In Europe, if you request directions to the bathroom, restroom, or washroom, you will be met with puzzled looks, so ask for the toilet or WC (water closet) instead. European toilets often have two flush buttons to choose from. Push the smaller button for liquid waste disposal and the larger one for everything else. While bidets are used as an alternative to toilet paper (See the Internet for information on how to use a bidet.), I still think their best use is to soak travel-weary feet.

BEST EUROPEAN CAR RENTAL SITES

CAR RENTAL COMPANIES

AutoEurope, Europcar, Kemwel, and Sixt are companies you have probably heard of because they have huge advertising budgets, but you may not be aware that they are consolidators. They say they scour the European car rental companies to find you the best price, but I have found that they sometimes add a hefty fee for their services. They are the middlemen, after all, and they must tack on an extra dollar amount for salaries and advertising budgets.

You may find you are far better off dealing directly with the car rental company, such as Avis or Hertz, itself. These companies have toll-free USA phone numbers, will be more inclined to help you in case of problems because they themselves made your reservation, and offer, especially if you join their free loyalty programs, a rate often two to three hundred dollars cheaper than the consolidators. Note, too, that online rates are much cheaper than telephone-generated rates.

Do not hesitate to use opaque sites like hotwire.com where the car rental company is not revealed until you commit to the transaction. You will probably find these companies list the cheapest prices in Europe. I have rented from Hotwire at least a dozen times and have always had a pleasant experience with a car from a reliable name brand company.

Car Insurance

Check with your credit card company before you leave home because they may tell you that handling the rental transaction with your credit card means you are covered by the credit card company's insurance. I have never had to purchase additional insurance.

Say "Cheese"

Always go over the rental car carefully to make sure you've noted all the dings and scratches. It's also a good idea to take photos with your digital camera or phone so you have proof of the imperfections that were there when you picked up the car.

DRIVING IN EUROPE

Route-Planning Websites - Two excellent resources for routes, whether you are driving, walking, or biking, are mappy and viamichelin. Both are similar in format to USA's Mapquest, but they deal, of course, with European roads. Here are a few other hints.

Highway numbers on maps are infrequently posted on road signs, but upcoming towns are almost always listed. Make sure you know what towns, both large and small, are on your route so you can steer in that direction. But don't forget the next tip.

Get GPS. This is the best tip I can give you. Either include GPS when you rent your car, download a positioning system before you leave home, (Navmii is one free app for your phone that I can recommend. It is highly rated and can be used offline.) or buy a navigation device before you leave home and download the necessary European maps.

Believe me when I say that I have driven Europe with and without its help so I know that having GPS makes your driving experience pleasant rather than frustrating.

Remember that if you're renting GPS along with the car, do not forget to ask the clerk to set the language to English. Make sure this is done and the GPS is functioning properly before you drive off the lot.

GPS will decipher directional road signs, find shortcuts when there are traffic jams, guide you through labyrinthine mazes masquerading as city streets, and warn you if you exceed the speed limit. In other words, if you're traveling with your spouse, it may well save your marriage. Don't turn the key in the ignition without it!

What's that Name?

Is it Florence or Firenze? Regardless of your mode of transportation, it's helpful to remember that some Americanized names for towns will not appear on maps or train schedules in the country itself. For example, in Italy, Genoa is Genova; Rome is Roma; Turin is Torino. To avoid problems, be certain you know how a city is identified in its own country.

Parking

Towns and cities in Europe use rectangular blue signs with a white "P" in the middle to indicate public parking. Don't forget to take your parking ticket with you when you exit the car. Usually there are no attendants at the lot, and you must pay your ticket at a machine which is often located far away from the parking lot itself. When you are ready to return to your car, look for the parking meter machine. Follow the instructions, pay the fee, take your receipt, and use it to exit the lot. You cannot leave the lot without that receipt.

The Passing Lane Is Really Just for Passing

In Europe, motorists do not hog the passing lane. Endear yourself to other drivers by using the passing lane only to pass. As soon as you've driven beyond the slower traffic, ease back in to the appropriate lane.

CREATE YOUR OWN PASSING LANE

In Mexico and Ireland, and perhaps other countries with narrow, two-lane major highways, the shoulder serves as a third lane, more or less. Don't panic when you're on a two-lane road and someone zooms up behind you and begins to pass. Ease off to the side, straddling the road and the shoulder, and let the anxious driver get on by.

EUROPEAN TOOL KIT

ACCESSING MONEY

Remember the good old days when your bank supplied you with travelers' checks which could be cashed just about anywhere in the world? Today, if you tried to cash a travelers' check in Europe, you'd have to go to a bank, wait at least a half hour, and, even then, might still be told that the bank was unable to cash your check.

Instead of that frustration, try this approach. Use a credit card wherever possible. You'll get the best exchange rate and low fees. By the way, if a merchant offers to translate his fee from euros into dollars before charging it to your card, do not do so. You will get a much better exchange rate if the charge is made in the local currency.

The second best way to access money is with an ATM (Automated Teller Machine) card that you can use at thousands of places throughout Europe. There will be a foreign transaction fee added by your bank, but this is still the best way to get your hands on euros.

Remember to tell both your credit card company and

your bank that you will be in Europe. This way they will know your card has not been stolen. Make sure that the daily limit you can withdraw using your ATM card is the maximum. You will not want to make several trips to the bank ATM when you can make one stop and get all the cash you need. Also double-check with your bank that your ATM card is recognized by the European ATM system.

To see what your dollar will be worth in euros before you leave home, check the xe.com site for the current exchange rates.

Unless you love paying exorbitant fees, do not order euros from your bank before your trip. When you arrive at the airport in Europe, head to the closest ATM machine and get the euros you need. The only caveat is to make sure you are using a bank-sponsored ATM as any other sort of ATM will give you a less desirable rate. Also, should anything negative occur, it is far easier to deal with a bank with many branches in foreign cities than to track down a currency company. By the way, in twenty years I've never had a problem with an ATM machine, so don't worry about this unduly. Also remember that before you head home, you should tuck a few euros away so you'll be prepared for your next trip.

ATM Tips

If possible, have your partner go with you for the ATM visit so he can provide a little more security as you're using the machine. And try to make those visits during banking hours. If the machine "eats" your card, it's a lot easier for one of you to go inside the bank to request help while the other person waits outside to make sure no one else tampers with the machine or your card.

All machines will give you the English language option so don't worry about understanding the directions. Do remember, though, that if your bank's limit is $500 a day, you will be able to request only €340 or so depending on the exchange rate. While the instructions are in English, the money is figured in that country's currency. Always get a receipt, be sure to count your money, and put it away securely before moving away from the ATM.

Understanding the Metric System

There's a natural antipathy between numbers and me. Try as I might, I don't understand them, and they do their best to outwit me whenever possible. Every time I think I have a handle on the slippery devils, they trip me up one way or another. Luckily, when traveling, I don't have to pin them down exactly in two areas; I'm not a stickler when it comes to mileage or temperature. If I can convert kilometers or Celsius in an easy-to-remember way and come relatively close to the actual number, that's good enough for me. That's why I'm a fan of the "close enough" method.

Number Confusion

Here's how it works. To convert kilometers into miles, I multiply the kilometers by six and drop the last digit. So, 50 kilometers times 6 equals 300. Drop the last digit and the answer is 30 miles. (If you went through a more complicated math equation, the absolutely correct answer, as opposed to the "close enough" answer, would be 31.06 miles.) If you've got 120 kilometers to drive before dinner, multiply 120 by 6 and get 720. Drop the last digit, and you realize you'll be stopping after only 72 miles (actually 74.56 miles). And if you're really hungry, doesn't that sound better than 120 km?

CELSIUS

The same approach works when converting Celsius temperatures to Fahrenheit. You could opt for an elaborate mathematical formula, which you'd never remember, or use "close enough." With my method, you double the Celsius number and add 32. So, 20 C doubled is 40 and when you add 32, the final answer is 72 F (Actually, if you used the complicated formula, the answer is 68 F.); 25 C becomes 82 F (actually 77 F); and 30 C is 92 F (actually 86 F). What's most interesting about this approach is that the method yields more accurate results in the lower range when it is imperative that you know the true temperature so you can dress appropriately, and less accurate temperatures when you are in the comfortable temperature range above 70F and won't suffer if you forget your sweater!

This "close enough" method has worked for me in Mexico as well as everywhere in Europe. Now, if only my bank would appreciate this approach to checkbook balancing, I'd be a completely happy woman!

KILOS VERSUS POUNDS

A kilo is 2.2 pounds (1000 grams) so half a kilo or even a quarter kilo will be the right amount of cold cuts to order from the deli clerk. Remember, when you are ordering in a European shop, use your thumb to indicate you want "one" of something. If you hold up only your index finger, you will get two items!

While we're on the subject of numbers, it's important to remember that some handwritten numbers in Europe are difficult to understand at first because they're not written like American numbers. The number one looks like a seven with bad posture but you can tell them apart because an actual seven will have a line through the long stem part of the numeral. Then there's the number four which looks like a sloppy nine. Until you get the hang of identifying numbers, you might want to ask for clarification when encountering any ones, sevens, fours or nines.

Another problem for Americans occurs with the decimal point and commas. Where we are accustomed to seeing a decimal point, the Europeans use a comma. Don't be alarmed when you see a loaf of bread for 1,50 as that's only one and a half euros; but don't try walking to a town 1.609 kilometers away because it's actually 1,609 kilometers, or a thousand miles, away!

Dates can also cause a problem because Europeans reverse the day and month in numbered dates. We celebrate Valentine's Day on 2-14-17 but that date would be written as 14-2-17 in Europe.

TIME CONFUSION

Europeans use the 24-hour clock, but it's not difficult to learn how to use it easily. From midnight until twelve noon, their time is measured like ours. You probably get up around 8:00 in the morning and so do a lot of Europeans. After noon, you add one number for each hour that passes. So, 1:00 p.m. in New York becomes 13:00 in Paris, 6:00 p.m. is 18:00 and so on. (An easy way to calculate any number in the teens is to simply subtract 12 to get "American" time. That means that 22:00 is 10:00 p.m.)

Time and Date

Check timeanddate.com for world time zones, calendars, and travel tools such as international dialing codes, distance calculator, and travel time calculator.

Weather

To see if you'll need to pack a sweater when you go to Paris or Rome or Madrid next spring, check climatezone.com.

Floors in Buildings

I often wonder if Europeans, who have many steps to climb because of ancient buildings with few elevators, try to comfort themselves by pretending there are fewer stairs than there really are. A six-story building in the USA has only five floors in Europe because the "first floor" is the "ground floor." So, remember, if your apartment is located on the first floor, you will climb a flight of stairs to get there, and if it's on the fourth floor, you may want to carry hiking gear for the five flights, or, better yet, find a different apartment with an elevator!

Securing your Valuables

For Men

On his first trip to Europe, David's greatest fear was being robbed. After weeks of research, he packed a neck pouch as well as a money belt, but both of them proved unsuitable for different reasons.

He used the neck pouch only two days because it chafed and added a strange protrusion to his chest. The cumbersome waist money belt didn't work much better. At the end of one long, exhausting day when he was reaching for the belt to pay for some dinner croissants, he found himself absent-mindedly undoing his jeans zipper while trying to get to his money. The money belt certainly kept his cash secure, but being arrested for indecent exposure would be too high a price to pay!

That night he developed a solution that worked beautifully for the rest of the trip. He inserted his belt in the cord that held the neck pouch and then wrapped the cord several times around his belt. (Use a belt that's the same color as the pouch cord if you can.) Making sure he left enough slack to allow easy use, he slipped the neck pouch deep into his front jeans pocket.

This technique worked beautifully. The pouch was easy to reach in David's front pocket, but it was secured by the looped-many-times-around-the-belt cord. Also, the unusual position (David usually carries a wallet in his back pocket.) was comfortable yet kept him aware of the wallet's whereabouts. I suppose a pickpocket could have tried to rip the wallet out of David's front pocket, but he would have had to drag a 6'5" man along with it! In the many trips since David perfected his secure technique for carrying valuables, he has never been mugged or lost a single euro.

For Women

I've tried neck pouches and waistband money belts and they made me miserable. I certainly didn't need an additional item dangling from my neck down to my mid-section or an extra item adding bulk at my waist. Those are two areas I absolutely do not want to call attention to at all!

Instead of pouches or belts, I carry one of two purses--either a lightweight but sturdy microfiber Ameribag with a dozen pockets and a strap that crosses over my chest or a Baggallini bag that is also cross-body with many pockets. Both are extremely versatile and can accommodate, in a pinch, an enormous amount of stuff. Both bags have withstood abuse for years and are still going strong.

If you feel the same way I do about pouches and belts, invest in a good microfiber bag or buy a Baggallini (frequently on sale at TJ Maxx) and don't worry about having your money stolen. As long as the bag's handle crosses your body with a sturdy strap, no one will be able to rip it off. In twenty years and dozens of trips, I have the same record as David--no muggings and no lost money.

Miscellaneous

Tips for Foodies

Since I know that "foodies" often use travel only as a means to fine dining, here is an alternative for cuisine connoisseurs. While I cannot recommend it for most Tightwads because it cuts so drastically into trip savings, if you are a gourmet who cannot imagine bypassing fine restaurants, you can still save some money on a trip by using a few tricks. Instead of assembling your meals as explained before, consider this approach.

Since breakfast is not a major meal in most European countries and seldom a culinary delight, save money--€10-30 per couple--by preparing this meal in your apartment. If you do not want to fix a simple egg and toast breakfast, pick up some pastries when you're out sightseeing. The next day, toss the pastries in your toaster oven, brew some coffee, and you will have a European breakfast for a fraction of a restaurant's charge.

You will find a restaurant's lunch menu to be quite similar to its dinner menu but at a significant discount. If you eat your main meal of the day in the early afternoon, you can save a lot of money.

Or, if you prefer to eat your dinner at a restaurant, buy lunch from a deli, refill your water bottle, and find a place to perch for a bit of people watching while you eat.

If nothing else, consider preparing drinks in your own apartment. A soda or cup of coffee in Europe is costly, well over €3.00, and liquor is double or triple that amount. Even if you only prepare your own drinks and eat every meal in a restaurant, you'll still save a bit of money.

Remember that the wait staff in European restaurants are well-paid and do not count on tips to round out their salaries. Because there's no particular need to provide excellent, fast service to earn tips, it may take much longer for your food to arrive than you might expect. Try to relax, enjoy the leisurely dining experience and do not worry about leaving a tip. Rounding the bill up is all that's necessary. Simply leave €19 for a lunch costing €18.50 or a single euro or two if you're feeling generous or received particularly good service.

ORDERING FREE WATER IN EUROPE

As a Tightwad following the suggestions in this book, you will not often find yourself in a restaurant. Still, if you cannot avoid it for one reason or another, keep your bill low by avoiding an expensive drink. It is the one item that needlessly increases the price of your meal. A soda, beer, or even bottled water in Europe will add €3-8 to a bill. A glass of water costs nothing and is healthier for you and your travel budget.

You will want to order water straight from the spigot. Here's what tap water is called in several countries: French: l'eau du robinet German: leitungswasser Italian: acqua del rubinetto Spanish: agua del grito Portuguese: agua de torneira.

By the way, if you're in Rome, don't hesitate to use the public water fountains called *nasonis* --"nose" because that's often the shape the fountains resemble. These ubiquitous fountains are a great way to fill your water bottle with clear, delicious spring water.

HOW TO RECOGNIZE THE BEST GELATO

After spending a month in Florence, where I believe I sampled gelato at every shop in town, I have learned how to distinguish genuine gelato, made with fresh ingredients, from the artificial variety.

Since there's an enormous taste difference between fresh and artificial, be sure to look for these qualities when choosing a gelato shop. Gelato made daily from fresh ingredients will usually be stored in covered bins and not displayed in mountainous swirls decorated with fruit or candy. Look carefully at the fruit flavors which should be subdued colors, not bright, neon ones. Banana gelato in particular is a good indicator of the shop's gelato in general. If it is a bright, glaring yellow that can only come from artificial, not fresh, ingredients, look for another shop.

SHOPPING IN EUROPE

In almost all European shops (large supermarkets are the exception), it is customary to greet the proprietor when entering the shop and to say good-bye when leaving. It's a very pleasant way to interact with people, and you'll enjoy the smile you'll share with the shopkeeper as much as he will. You will be considered rude if you forget these fundamental amenities, so remember to use Fodor's free Language for Travelers website to learn the foreign words you will need.

BUY FLOWERS

Not only is it fun to feel like a native when you purchase an inexpensive bouquet of flowers from a street vendor, but the flowers will add a lovely grace note to your apartment.

HOW TO MAKE PHONE CALLS

After searching twenty minutes for a shop that sold phone cards and then wrestling for another fifteen minutes with the telephone that only "spoke" Spanish, I am convinced that Skype is the easiest, cheapest, and best way to make phone calls within Europe.

Skype is a voice-over program that is free to download to your computer. Minutes of inexpensive calling time (around 2-3 cents per minute) are pre-paid with your credit card so all you need do is "dial" the number using your Skype keypad (It appears on your computer when you're ready to make a call.) If you need more help, there are many tutorials on You-Tube that will show you exactly how to use this easy system.

If you prefer a cell phone, I've been told that you can get the information you need from your carrier (T-Mobile, Verizon, etc.) to "unlock" your phone, buy a SIMS card in Europe, and enjoy prepaid dialing overseas.

PHONE HOME

Consider using a Republic Wireless phone as your smartphone if you will need to make frequent phone calls from Europe to the States. They are ranked number one by *Consumer Reports* magazine, have some of the cheapest data plans (I average $12 a month for everything.) and you can use Wi-Fi to call the States for free while you're in Europe.

PREVENT LEAKING PENS

I'm persnickety about pens. While ballpoints may have their advantages, no one could ever tear me away from my gel cartridge pens. I love the way the ink flows over the paper, and, when I use them, I swear my words flow more easily too.

The only problem with gel pens is that they don't always travel well. The cartridges are sensitive to the changes in cabin pressure and seem to "explode" after a flight. There's nothing worse than uncapping a beloved pen when you're ready to sign a receipt and having it leak all over your hand.

The Pilot pen people have a solution. The package for their "real fountain pen" (and it does perform just like a fountain pen!) provides this helpful hint: "When using most liquid ink pens on an airplane, be sure to remove the cap with the point upward to avoid problems that could occur due to cabin pressure."

DON'T FORGET TO SAVE THE MEMORIES

Because you are traveling like a Tightwad, your senses are on high alert and you're savoring everything you see, hear and smell. Make a note about the way the Ponte Vecchio Bridge turns golden at sunset or how the pigeons call to one another with their throaty coos in Paris. Don't forget to record the yeasty aroma of freshly baked bolillos in Spain. Write a passage describing the way the morning mists modestly shroud King Ludwig's castles from the encroaching sun in Bavaria, Germany. Whether it's a paragraph or a page, write a journal entry every day so you don't forget. After all, these are the memories you will want to keep for a lifetime.

ACKNOWLEDGMENTS

Thanks to Boydo and Tomas who traveled many a mile with me; to Maureen who was never at a loss for words; to Kevin who gave my ideas shape; and to David, always to David.

ABOUT THE AUTHOR

Dru Pearson fell in love with travel when her parents took her to Camp Corbly when she was three months old. She's suffered from wanderlust ever since.

Recent trips are recorded on her Tightwad Travel blog, http://tightwadtravel.blogspot.com/.

Her books are available on Amazon and Barnes & Noble.

Europe on a Dime: Five-Star Travel on a One-Star Budget

https://www.amazon.com/Europe-Dime-Five-Star-One-Star-Tightwad/dp/1470172526

http://www.barnesandnoble.com/w/europe-on-a-dime-dru-pearson/1111390683?type=eBook

Retire in Mexico--Live Better for Less Money
https://www.amazon.com/Retire-Mexico-Better-American-shoestring-ebook/dp/B003YOSCJA

http://www.barnesandnoble.com/w/retire-in-mexico-live-better-for-less-money-live-the-american-dream-in-mexico-for-half-the-price-luxury-on-a-shoestring-can-be-yours-dru-pearson/1113655001?ean=9781496154040

Made in the USA
Monee, IL
20 November 2022

18153348R00092